GRACE IN THE END

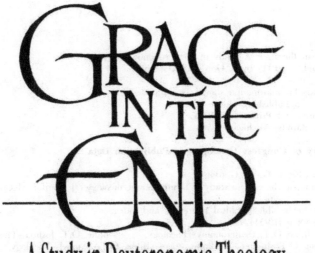

GRACE IN THE END

A Study in Deuteronomic Theology

J. Gordon McConville

ZondervanPublishingHouse
Academic and Professional Books
Grand Rapids, Michigan

A Division of HarperCollins*Publishers*

FOR

Alistair, Carys, Andrew, and Claire

HB 02.16.2023

Grace in the End: A Study of Deuteronomic Theology
Copyright © 1993 by J. Gordon McConville

Requests for information should be addressed to:
Zondervan Publishing House
Academic and Professional Books
Grand Rapids, Michigan 49530

Library of Congress Cataloging-in-Publication Data

McConville, J. G. (J. Gordon)
    Grace in the end : a study of Deuteronomic theology / J. Gordon McConville.
        p.   cm.
    Includes bibliographical references and index.
    ISBN 0-310-51421-5
    1. Bible. O.T. Deuteronomy–Theology.   2. Bible. O.T. Joshua–Theology.
3. Bible. O.T. Judges–Theology.   4. Bible. O.T. Samuel–Theology.   5.
Bible. O.T. Kings–Theology.   I. Title.   II. Title: Deuteronomic Theology.
    BS1285.5.M33   1993
    230–dc20   92-27036
                                                                                    CIP

Edited by Verlyn D. Verbrugge
Cover design by Dennis Hill

Printed in the United States of America

◆ Contents ◆

◆ Abbreviations ◆

ad loc.	In a commentary, under the verse discussed
AB	Anchor Bible
ANET	*Ancient Near Eastern Texts* (by Pritchard)
CBQ	*Catholic Biblical Quarterly*
BA	*Biblical Archaeologist*
Dtr	The Deuteronomist
DtH	The Deuteronomic History
EVV	English Versions of the Bible
HKAT	Handkommentar zum alten Testament
Ibid.	Same book as the previous one cited
ICC	International Critical Commentary
IEJ	*Israel Exploration Journal*
JSOT	*Journal for the Study of the Old Testament*
JSOTSup	Journal for the Study of the Old Testament Supplement
KHAT	Kurzer Handkommentar zum alten Testament
MT	Masoretic Text
NCB	New Century Bible
NICOT	New International Commentary on the Old Testament
NT	New Testament
OT	Old Testament
OTL	Old Testament Library
SBLDS	Society of Biblical Literature Dissertation Series
SJT	*Scottish Journal of Theology*
SN	Succession Narrative
SVT	Supplements to *Vetus Testamentum*
TB	*Tyndale Bulletin*
TOTC	Tyndale Old Testament Commentary
VT	*Vetus Testamentum*
Urdt	Urdeuteronomium (hypothetical original Deuteronomy)
WBC	Word Biblical Commentary
WBT	Word Biblical Themes
ZAW	*Zeitschrift für die alttestamentliche Wissenschaft*

◆ Preface to Series ◆

The editors are pleased to announce the "Studies in Old Testament Biblical Theology" series, with the hope that it contributes to the field of Old Testament theology and stimulates further discussion. If Old Testament theology is the queen of Old Testament studies, she is a rather neglected queen. To write in the area of Old Testament theology is a daunting proposition, one that leads many to hesitate taking on the task. After all, Old Testament theology presupposes an understanding of all the books of the Old Testament and, at least as conceived in the present project, an insight into its connection with the New Testament.

Another reason why theology has been neglected in recent years is simply a lack of confidence that the Old Testament can be summarized in one or even a number of volumes. Is there a center, a central concept, under which the entire Old Testament may be subsumed? Many doubt it. Thus, while a number of articles, monographs, and commentaries address the theology of a source, a chapter, or even a book, few studies address the Old Testament as a whole.

The editors of this series also believe it is impossible to present the entirety of the Old Testament message under a single rubric. Even as important a concept as the covenant fails to incorporate all aspects of the Old Testament (note especially wisdom literature). Thus, this series will present separate volumes, each devoted to different theme, issue, or perspective of biblical theology, and will show its importance for the Old Testament and for the entire Christian canon.

One last word needs to be said about theological approach. Gone are the days when scholars, especially those who work in a field as ideologically sensitive as theology, can claim neutrality by hiding behind some kind of scientific methodology. It is, therefore, important to announce the approach taken in this series. Those who know the editors, authors, and publisher will not be surprised to learn that an evangelical approach is taken throughout this series. At the same time, however, we believe that those who do not share this starting point may still benefit and learn from these studies.

The present volume is the first in the series and is an example of what the editors have hoped to accomplish. After defining the term, Gordon McConville skillfully considers the basic aspects of Deuteronomic theology: the revelation of Israel's God in word and in history, election and covenant, God's grace, and a hope beyond the exile of Israel. Deuteronomy presents the importance of knowing God, of living by grace, and of living responsibly in his presence. The tension between law and grace has not been reduced by the coming of the Lord Jesus Christ and by the inclusion of the Gentiles into the covenant community. As McConville argues, the relation between the testaments is not one of contrast, but of growth and development.

The general editors of this series, Willem A. VanGemeren and Tremper Longman III, wish to thank the academic publishing department of Zondervan, particularly Stan Gundry and Verlyn Verbrugge, who will be working most closely with the series.

Willem A. VanGemeren
Professor of Old Testament and Semitic Languages
Trinity Evangelical Divinity School

◆ 1 ◆

Introduction

DEFINING DEUTRONOMIC THEOLOGY

Deuteronomy is one of the great theological documents of the Bible, or of any time. The mere fact that Jesus quotes more often from it than from any other book of the Old Testament is perhaps a sufficient invitation to a study of its theology. Its effect on his mind is also a symptom of its massive importance in forming the thinking of ancient Israel and in serving as backdrop to many of the discussions in later Judaism. As the final book of the Pentateuch and the great Mosaic invitation to life in covenant with Yahweh, it breaks free from its moorings in tribal, agricultural Israel—though that milieu breathes through its motley laws—and goes to the heart of the great issues of the relationship between God and human beings.

The very term "Deuteronomic Theology," the subject of the present volume, bears witness to the influence of Deuteronomy itself. It suggests a whole body of theological discourse, identified both by subject-matter and style, as characteristic of the book that stimulated it. And indeed, modern scholarship posits just such a body within the Old Testament, contained not just in particular books but pervasively, so that its ultimate limits continue as a matter of scholarly discussion and permanently await definition.

Herein, of course, lies a methodological problem that will necessarily concern us as we try to penetrate to the heart of "Deuteronomic Theology." It is clear from what has been said already that the latter term is not simply equivalent to "the theology of Deuteronomy." Rather, it asks us to understand, not the root only, but the root and branches together.

One of the main problems, however, is to know what is root and what is branch. Our task would be straightforward if we could assume that the root was the book of Deuteronomy, no more and no less, and the branches were other OT books that we could suppose were later in time and took up themes of the former. Such a procedure is inadequate, however, since it fails to take account of most of what has been written on the subject, and since most writers, ultimately under the influence of de Wette and Wellhausen, take a significantly different view of matters.

In the attempt to distinguish root from branch in Deuteronomic theology, the lines of the debate were laid down by Wellhausen. Building on the work of de Wette, he argued that in an early form, Deuteronomy originated in the context of King Josiah's reform of religion in the late seventh century B.C. This Proto-Deuteronomy (Wellhausen's *Urdeuteronomium* [Urdt]) was expanded to meet new conditions, especially in the exile, until the present form of the book took shape.

Here, then, is a different scenario from the one in which the book as a whole is taken simply as the source of influence. It involves historical, literary, and theological criteria, on the basis of which the development of Deuteronomic theology is reconstructed, not only within Deuteronomy but in other books. Chief among the latter are those that make up the so-called Deuteronomic (or Deuteronomistic) History (DtH), namely, Joshua, Judges, 1, 2 Samuel and 1, 2 Kings. In the classic theory of the composition of DtH, perpetrated by M. Noth,[1] the present form of Deuteronomy is attributable to an exilic author, the "Deuteronomist" (Dtr), who cast the already existing Urdt into a historical framework. He wrote this revised book as the beginning of his history of Israel and Judah, using older sources, in order to explain the downfall of Judah in terms of judgment for breach of the covenant.

In Noth's scheme of things, therefore, the distinction between root and branch is conceived as that between "Deuteronomic" (i.e., deriving from Urdt) and "Deuteronomistic" (deriving from an exilic revision). When matters are understood in this way, clearly the interpreter's major task is to try to define the character and content of Urdt. In terms of the theory, however, this is an extremely delicate task, because it involves a dialectic between the data observable in Deuteronomy itself and the theory. No doubt this is a kind of circle that much reading of the OT inevitably runs into. However, the interpreter should be sensitive to the possibility that the theory might unduly dominate the reconstruction of the authentic Deuteronomy.

I believe that this has in fact often happened, partly because certain theological value-judgments have been brought to bear that lack adequate justification either in Deuteronomy itself or in OT theology more generally. For example, the distinction between root and branch has often been made on the basis of a polarization of the theological themes of law and grace.

Our aim in the pages that follow will be to try to characterize Deuteronomic theology on the basis of secure literary, historical, and theological criteria. I shall anticipate some of the argument by saying at the outset that I believe that Deuteronomy as we have it today is the true formative influence, not only on DtH, but more generally on OT

---

[1]M. Noth, *The Deuteronomistic History*, JSOTSup 15 (Sheffield: JSOT, 1981).

theology. This view attributes to the book a vigor and brilliance of thought that is rarely appreciated. It sees it as a document of theological profundity, capable of discerning a range of possibilities in the relationship between God and human beings, rather than as a series of layered programs for ever-new situations.

This does not mean, however, that "Deuteronomic Theology" is simply an exposition of the theology of Deuteronomy. Part of our task is to explore the books that relate most closely and overtly to DtH (Jos–2Ki). These books, though they may appropriately be called "Deuteronomic," do not repeat or invoke that book in any simple way. Rather, they have their own individuality and character. In this respect they may be compared with the book of Jeremiah, which, as I have shown elsewhere, shows a profound knowledge of Deuteronomy while making a theological contribution of its own.[2] It is important to identify such distinctions—it is in these terms, indeed, that we can properly speak about the root and the branches. Yet the debt of the books of DtH to Deuteronomy should not be underestimated. Indeed, their capacity to generate new statements, such as we find in them, is part of DtH's power.

"GRACE IN THE END": THE RELEVANCE OF DEUTERONOMIC THEOLOGY

The writing of the present volume has not been motivated by a desire to nitpick about sources and verselets. It is written from a conviction about the relevance of biblical theology in our world. A belief in the vital contribution of the Old Testament to that theology is shared, I suppose, by all the authors in the present series and certainly represents my own view. In my opinion, Deuteronomy, with its associated

---

[2] J. G. McConville, *Judgment and Promise: Interpreting the Book of Jeremiah* (Winona Lake, Ind.: Eisenbrauns/Leicester: Inter-Varsity, 1993).

literature, has a special place in constructing any OT theology. With its highly distinctive style and deceptive simplicity, it contains a powerful yet subtle theology of history. Yet it is not grandiose or idealistic (in the sense of abstract and theoretical). Rather it is human and practical. Above all, however, it is a document of faith, faith that has come to terms with the realities of the world, often harsh and painful, and affirms gladly that God, the author of all life, desires to bless his people.

The present volume was written in the aftermath of the revolutionary events in Eastern Europe that have resulted in the end of Communist rule there. While many of the immediate consequences of that series of events have been bitter (painful adjustments in Germany, all-out war in Yugoslavia), there remains something thrilling and captivating about the sight of the Berlin wall being dismantled and the exuberance of the Germans celebrating the end of a horrifying, deadening tyranny. The failure of the coup in Moscow in the face of the courage of Boris Yeltsin and fellow-reformers was another moment that was laden with significance for human history. Yet, significant as these things were in themselves, they seemed to point even beyond their immediate parameters and to say something about the realities that underlie human life in God's world.

Bishop Stephen Sykes, reflecting on the events in Berlin in 1989, wrote: "There is grace in history in the end."[3] Here was a faith-perspective on contemporary events. It was not unduly euphoric, as if the troubles of the world had been swept away in a moment. But it recognized that the hand of God, who has revealed the end of all things in the resurrection of Christ and will finally bring his kingdom to pass in the world, may also be seen in every defeat of the forces of evil and in every deliverance of human beings from that which

---

[3]In "The Truth Has Set Eastern Europe Free," *The Independent*, (Dec. 28, 1989).

crushes the spirit. The present volume takes its title from Bishop Sykes' remark.

METHOD OF PROCEDING

From our opening paragraphs, it will be clear that we cannot proceed immediately to a description of Deuteronomic theology. We must begin by addressing the literary and historical questions that have become so much a part of the attempt to understand the book itself. To do so will by no means be to digress on to a mere byway, for in taking this route the heart of Deuteronomic concerns will gradually be exposed. Our final statement of the essential features of Deuteronomic theology will draw much from these explorations and would hardly be possible without them.

◆ 2 ◆

The Deuteronomic Idea in Biblical Scholarship

The aim of the present chapter is to explore the character of Deuteronomic theology as it is understood in modern scholarship. This exercise will be largely descriptive, though we shall try to show what kinds of assumptions are made when Deuteronomic theology is characterized. A critique of the approaches will be the subject of the following chapter.

The attempt to describe Deuteronomic theology is governed by three factors: First, the link that may reasonably be made between the setting or origin of Deuteronomy and its meaning; second, the difficulty of establishing its setting (if a Mosaic authorship is not presupposed) in any particular period in Israel's history on internal grounds alone; and third, its theological elusiveness. The last of these derives from the fact that the book holds together ideas that can appear contradictory, such as law and grace. The reticence or ambiguity of the book about its own setting and meaning constitutes the greatest difficulty in its interpretation. We shall see how interpreters have evaluated it differently as a result.

Modern critical study of Deuteronomy is generally traced to W. M. L. de Wette, who proposed in 1805 a close association of the book with King Josiah's reform of the national religion of Judah in 621 B.C., Deuteronomy being identified with the "Book of the Law" in 2 Kings 22:8.[1] J. Wellhausen went on to argue that it was an early form of the book (Urdt) that gave the reform its impetus.[2]

For Wellhausen, Urdt was a law-code, consisting of Deuteronomy 12–26; this view has remained influential, even if opinions have varied as to its exact extent and whether or not it was originally furnished with an introduction.[3] He explained the purpose of this original Deuteronomy in connection with Josiah's reform, maintaining that the reform was an important turning-point in Israel's religious history and that Urdt, correspondingly, marked a mid-point in her theological and literary development. The "centralization" of Judah's worship in Jerusalem, put in place by Josiah, was a decisive step away from the permissiveness that had reigned hitherto in religious practice. Wellhausen regarded this earlier freedom in religion as a good thing, since it was spontaneous and relatively unburdened by cultic ordinance and priestly control. For him, Josiah's centralization tended to constrict and formalize religion through many regulations.[4]

In this reconstruction, Deuteronomy's law regarding worship was its most telling and characteristic feature.

[1]W. M. L. de Wette, *Dissertatio critico-exegetica qua Deuteronomium a prioribus pentateuchi libris diversum, alius cuiusdam recentioris auctoris opus esse monstratur* (Jena, 1805).

[2]J. Wellhausen, *Prolegomena to the History of Ancient Israel* (Edinburgh: A. and C. Black, 1885), 279–80.

[3]J. Wellhausen, *Die Composition des Hexateuchs und der historischen Bücher des alten Testaments*, 2d ed. (Berlin: Georg Reimer, 1889), 189–195. In subsequent discussion, it became common to suppose that the legal section did indeed have an introduction, namely 4:44–11:32; see S. R. Driver, *A Critical and Exegetical Commentary on Deuteronomy*, ICC (Edinburgh: T. and T. Clark, 1895), lxv; G. W. Anderson, *A Critical Introduction to the Old Testament* (London: Duckworth, 1959), 44; G. Fohrer, *Introduction to the Old Testament* (London: SPCK, 1970), 171. Driver also included ch. 28 (p. lxvii). M. Noth defined Urdt as "essentially" 4:44–30:20; see his *The Deuteronomistic History* (Sheffield: JSOT, 1981), 16.

[4]Wellhausen, *Prolegomena*, 17–38 (51).

Wellhausen held that it was Josiah's understanding of the command of Deuteronomy 12:5 ("you are to seek the place the LORD your God will choose from among all your tribes to put his Name there for his dwelling") that convinced him of the need to centralize public worship in Jerusalem and to regard all other sacred places as idolatrous (cf. 12:3). Many of Deuteronomy's laws, in fact, could be understood as revisions of existing legislation, designed precisely to enforce this centralization. Wellhausen's primary evidence for this view lay in the frequent repetition of the formula concerning "the place the LORD your God will choose," and the related expression "before the LORD."[5]

Wellhausen increased the potency of his argument by contending that certain of the regulations about worship were modified greatly in order to bring Israelite practices into line with the policy of centralization. The laws of the tithe (14:22–29) and the feasts (16:1–17) illustrate the point. Only in Deuteronomy does the law of the tithe require attendance at the central sanctuary, and the location of the Passover meal there (16:2) is particularly striking in view of its character elsewhere as a family feast.[6] Only at one point did Josiah fail to implement the laws of Deuteronomy, namely, his refusal to allow the "priests of the high places" to stand alongside the Jerusalem priests in the new order (2Ki 23:9). Even this feature of Josiah's measures, however, seemed to be the

---

[5]The "place-formula" occurs at 12:5, 11, 14, 18; 14:23, 25; 15:20; 16:2, 6–7, 15–16; 17:8; 18:6; 26:2. In addition, the phrase "before the LORD" occurs 17 times, effectively meaning, with few exceptions (24:4, 13), "at the place which the LORD will choose."

[6]Contrast Deuteronomy law of the tithe with Nu 18:20–25. Other legislation on the feasts occurs at Ex 23:14–17; Lev 23; Nu 28–29. For the Passover see also Ex 12–13. See also Driver, *Deuteronomy*, 166–73 (on the tithe), and p. 192 on the Passover: "The Passover loses consequently, in some degree, its old character . . . of a domestic rite"; cf. also M. Weinfeld, "The Emergence of the Deuteronomic Movement: The Historical Antecedents," in *Das Deuteronomium: Entstehung, Gestalt und Botschaft*, ed. N. Lohfink (Leuven: Leuven Univ. Press, 1965), 95.

exception that proves the rule, because of the supposition that the passage in 2 Kings referred expressly to the law of Deuteronomy 18:6–8.[7] Wellhausen's synthesis proved attractive to many and spawned a number of detailed attempts to define more precisely the Deuteronomic adaptation of older laws in terms of the centralization of Israel's worship.[8]

THE PURPOSE OF URDT

Our present interest, however, is not with historical or literary critical questions in themselves, but rather with the understanding of Urdt that lies behind them. If Wellhausen is right in thinking that it was essentially a law-code produced for Josiah's new order to be brought in by his reform, then our "Deuteronomic Theology" will have to be stated in terms of law.

The story of the study of Deuteronomy, however, was to take new turns, leading to different appraisals. Chief among these has been the tendency to separate the composition of the book from the time of Josiah's reform itself. While it is still widely dated to the seventh century, the question has become more open as to its occasion and milieu, and consequently its original purpose. The Josianic dating, admittedly, continues to be defended by some.[9] On the other hand, an earlier dating

---

[7]Wellhausen, *Prolegomena*, 124. I have shown elsewhere the error of associating these two passages in this way, as have others; see my *Law and Theology in Deuteronomy* (Sheffield: JSOT, 1984), 132–35; cf. M. Haran, *Temples and Temple Service in Ancient Israel* (Oxford: Oxford Univ. Press, 1978), 99–100.

[8]For example, see F. Horst, *Das Privilegrecht Jahves* (Göttingen: Vandenhoeck and Ruprecht, 1930); R. P. Merendino, *Das deuteronomische Gesetz* (Bonn: P. Hanstein, 1969). See also the commentaries of S. R. Driver (*Deuteronomy*) and C. Steuernagel (*Deuteronomium und Josua*, HKAT [Göttingen: Vandenhoeck and Ruprecht, 1900]).

[9]R. E. Clements, defending this dating against the allegation that the book must thus be seen as a "pious fraud," argues that its authors composed it "to safeguard something in Israel's life that they felt to be indispensable and ancient" (*Deuteronomy* OT Guides [Sheffield: JSOT, 1989], 70–71).

fits with the belief that a "reform movement" was in place well before Josiah's time, a view that has support from the history of the monarchy of Judah in 1, 2 Kings.[10] Historically too, it is plausible that a conservative movement (such as might propagate Deuteronomy) must have arisen as a reaction against the idolatrous measures espoused by King Manasseh during his long reign in the early part of the century (686–42 B.C.).[11] Others have suggested the even earlier reform in the reign of Hezekiah, a reformer in the style of his descendant Josiah.[12]

It is fair to say, then, that scholarship since Wellhausen has tended to look to the seventh century as a whole for the origins of Deuteronomy rather than narrowly at Josiah's reform. It was a century of massive upheaval and uncertainty in Judah. Its neighbor Israel, the larger part of the ancient covenant people, had fallen to the new imperial power of Assyria in 721 B.C., and Judah itself had almost followed when King Sennacherib laid waste its fortified cities and stood at the gates of a despairing Jerusalem, only to be reprieved by a miraculous intervention (2Ki 18:13–19:37). Judah survived, and Hezekiah's reform represented a bold assertion of independence. Yet Judah was henceforth in thrall to the Assyrian overlord, as Hezekiah's own compromises (2Ki 18:16) and Manasseh's policy of total submission (21:1–6) made clear. The trauma of the fall of the north, followed by the temporary hopes aroused by Hezekiah and then the humiliations endured under Manasseh, must have caused great heart-searching among the faithful people of Judah. In this context scholars have increasingly sought the origin and

---

[10]See 1Ki 15:9–15; 22:41–44; 2Ki 12:2–8; 18:1–8. For a detailed treatment of this aspect of Kings, see H.-D. Hoffmann, *Reform und Reformen: Untersuchungen zu einem Grundthema der deuteronomistischen Geschichtsschreibung* (Zurich: Theologischer Verlag, 1980); see also McConville, "Narrative and Meaning in the Books of Kings," *Biblica* 70 (1989), and further below.

[11]So Driver, *Deuteronomy*, xlix–lv.

[12]M. Weinfeld, "Deuteronomic Movement," 91. He does, however, allow for elaboration in the time of Josiah.

purpose of Deuteronomy, a context that allows for some variation in the appraisals of the purpose of the book. In fact, for many scholars the book is no longer seen as a new invention, but a reassertion of ancient values.

DEUTERONOMY: LAW OR GOSPEL?

In their attempt to discover the earliest origins of Deuteronomy, a number of influential scholars took the view that it was not essentially a product of Judah at all, but rather of the old northern Israel. A. Alt believed that it was composed there some time after the fall of Samaria.[13] H. Wolff and G. von Rad thought that Levites living in country areas of the northern kingdom were the bearers of the old traditions that eventually found their deposit in Deuteronomy.[14] Such an understanding of the origin of Deuteronomy already suggests a restorationist and revivalist purpose, implying an assertion of the wholeness of Israel—a bold stroke in the circumstances of the imminent (or actual) demise of the northern kingdom.[15]

The theory as von Rad developed it is a particularly good example of how an understanding of origins leads to an interpretation of the book. For him, Deuteronomy was born and nurtured in the worship of Israel. Its form closely resembles that of the annual covenant renewal ceremony that von Rad believed happened at Shechem from Israel's earliest

---

[13]A. Alt, "Die Heimat des Deuteronomiums," in *Kleine Schriften zur Geschichte des Volkes Israel* (Munich: C. H. Beck'sche Verlagsbuchhandlung, 1953), 2:250–51.

[14]H. Wolff, "Hoseas geistige Heimat," in *Gesammelte Studien zum alten Testament* (Munich: Kaiser Verlag, 1964), 248–50; G. von Rad, *Studies in Deuteronomy* (London: SCM, 1953), 40–41, 60ff. For the latter, this accounted for the book's evident interest in the welfare of the Levites (14:29; 18:6–8) and for its Holy War ideology.

[15]Von Rad had identified the theme of the unity of Israel as a central part of the program of Deuteronomy in an early work, *Das Gottesvolk* (Stuttgart: Kohlhammer, 1929).

days in the land and that was based on the Sinai covenantal traditions.[16] Deuteronomy, therefore, derives from the ceremony; thus it included a presentation of the events at Sinai with associated paranetic material (in chs. 1–11), a reading of the law (12:1–26:15), the sealing of the covenant (26:16–19), and blessings and curses (27–33).[17]

The relationship between the ceremony and the book is complex, however. To von Rad, Deuteronomy is not the earliest deposit of the preaching of the ceremony; this is found in Exodus 19–24.[18] Deuteronomy itself "is less close to the actual cultic situation."[19] Indeed, it has developed so far from it that it has also absorbed the main elements of the quite distinct ancient festival of Gilgal, the one that celebrated the Exodus from Egypt and settlement in the land.[20] This separate set of traditions, which in his view conspicuously lacked any stress on the revelation of the law, included the promises to the patriarchs, the Exodus from Egypt, the Holy War, and the gift of the land of Canaan.[21] These themes were summed up in what von Rad called the Short Historical Credos of Deuteronomy 6:20–24 and 26:5b–9.[22]

In other words, whereas Shechem's Sinai tradition stressed law, Gilgal's traditions featured election and promise. In fully incorporating both, Deuteronomy gives, in von Rad's view, a distinctive treatment of the wide range of Israel's ancient traditions. Reflecting theologically on this achievement, he writes: "The blending of the two traditions

---

[16]Von Rad, "The Form-Critical Problem of the Hexateuch," in *The Problem of the Hexateuch and Other Essays* (London: SCM, 1984), 36–38.

[17]Ibid., 27; cf. his *Studies in Deuteronomy*, 14.

[18]Von Rad, "The Problem of the Hexateuch," 27–28.

[19]Ibid., 28.

[20]In literary-critical terms, this happened when the Sinai traditions were built into the Hexateuchal Exodus-Settlement narrative; see ibid., 53–54.

[21]Von Rad, *Studies in Deuteronomy*, 45–55.

[22]Von Rad, "The Problem of the Hexateuch," 3–6.

gives definition to the two fundamental propositions of the whole message of the Bible: Law and Gospel."[23]

In another place, however, von Rad notes how the latter idea (Gospel standing close to election and promise) gains a certain primacy in Deuteronomy. Yahweh's offer of election to Israel is "without tension," because it is "all-sufficient." He goes on:

> There is no need on man's part to seek, or to strive by means of religious works which might or might not achieve their purpose, to compel salvation and partake in it.[24]

Here, the element of command is allowed its place, of course, but obedience to it is firmly regarded as a consequence of election. Indeed, "this question of obedience, that is, its possibilities and limits, are no problem at all for Deuteronomy."[25] On the other hand, those parts of the book that sound the legal note most strongly are late and secondary.[26] The overriding purpose of Deuteronomy, therefore, is a proclamation of the present reality of Yahweh's saving presence with his people. This, we may note, is a far cry from Wellhausen's assessment of it as a law-book, produced in the context of Josiah's reform.

Before drawing further conclusions from von Rad's treatment of Deuteronomy, it will help our study to compare briefly the interpretation of E. W. Nicholson, one that is similar yet distinct. Nicholson agrees with von Rad in seeking the origins of Deuteronomy in the worship of ancient Israel (for him the Autumn festival of Covenant Renewal) rather than in immediate dependence on Josiah's reform.[27] However, he repudiates von Rad's programmatic separation both

---

[23]Ibid., 54.

[24]Von Rad, *Studies in Deuteronomy*, 71.

[25]Ibid., 72.

[26]Ibid.

[27]E. W. Nicholson, *Deuteronomy and Tradition* (Oxford: Blackwell, 1967), 15, 40.

of Exodus and Sinai traditions and of the theologies of Gospel and Law, for three reasons. First, both elements are in fact in the Shechem covenantal tradition as recorded in Joshua 24.[28] second, the treaty-form of Deuteronomy (unknown to von Rad when he wrote) favoured the close association of election and covenantal command.[29] Finally, Nicholson introduces a theological criterion of his own when he says that "to separate the election theme from the covenant robs the latter of all motivation."[30]

While von Rad and Nicholson each find room in Deuteronomy for both law and promise (or Gospel), there is a subtle distinction between them in their final appraisal of the book. Von Rad's proclamation of election and promise connects with the roller-coaster events of the seventh century in a very particular way, as a celebration of the bright hopes that were associated with the deliverance from Sennacherib and the reprieve of the reforming Hezekiah. For him, Deuteronomy is a call to believe the promise, even if the need for obedience is also recognized. Nicholson, on the other hand, finds the call to obedience more prominent; the book has an urgent, prophetic ring to it, because it knows that the danger to the people of God is still real.

Our study of von Rad and comparison with Nicholson illustrate three factors in the reading of Deuteronomy. First, a close connection exists between a scholar's theory about the book's origins and his/her theological appraisal of it. Wellhausen, von Rad, and Nicholson may all be contrasted in this respect. second, Deuteronomy subtly blends themes that might be regarded as opposites (Law and Gospel/election/grace). The book's suppleness, even elusiveness, of thought in this area is no doubt one reason for the different theological interpretations that it has attracted.[31] Finally,

---

[28]Ibid., 42.

[29]Ibid., 43–44.

[30]Ibid., 42.

[31]We shall return to the law-grace topic more fully in the next chapter.

however, we have seen how much interpretation can be affected by the theological world of the interpreter himself. In von Rad's case, for example, this relationship is illustrated by his preference for Gospel over Law, and indeed by his apology for the presence in Deuteronomy of any requirement of obedience. The combination of the latter two factors (the book's ambiguity and the interpreter's theological preferences) is potent, and while the last one is in a sense unavoidable, any reader of the Bible needs to be aware of the excessive role that it can play.

CONSERVATIVE OR RADICAL?

Our search thus far for the essential spirit of the original Deuteronomy has moved in the orbit of the theological topic of law and grace. This, however, is only one part of the theological thematic of Deuteronomy. Quite as important is the question whether the book is at heart a conservative, pro-establishment document, or on the contrary a deeply radical writing. Both views have been espoused in scholarly treatments.

Exegetically, Deuteronomy's law concerning the king (17:14–20) has been drafted on both sides. This has been possible partly because only in this short passage is the topic directly addressed, and partly because its terms may be read positively (since the institution of kingship is actually permitted) or negatively (since it is laid under solemn constraints: the king must be as one among brothers and a student of the law of God, and he must not exploit his position for personal gain). Also relevant is the so-called centralization law (12:5, 11, 14, etc.), requiring that Israel worship "at the place the LORD your God will choose." Like the section on the king, this one can be read either as strongly supportive of the official cult or as an attempt to bring it under control so as to change it completely. It is best to reserve comment on these exegetical issues until we have put the discussion in a broader context.

The question whether Deuteronomy aims to preserve or to undermine the status quo centers on the interpretation of its attitude to the king and to the organization of worship. On one side of the argument lies what some see as the strong association between the book itself and the Jerusalem/Davidic traditions. Indeed, Josiah's reform can be seen as a reaffirmation of Yahweh's promise to David of an everlasting dynasty that would reign from Zion, Yahweh's own "holy hill." This set of ideas, in which the king enjoys a special relationship with Yahweh within his covenant with Israel, receives its historical explanation in 2 Samuel 7 and is celebrated in such Psalms as 2; 45; 48; 72; 76; 89; 110; 132. These ideas have sometimes been regarded as representing a "sacral" theology, in which the relationship between God and Israel was thought to depend somehow on the existence and maintenance of king and cult, two institutions quite distinct from Israel's covenantal traditions.[32] If a king of Judah could promulgate measures, based on Deuteronomy, to concentrate the nation's religious life in the capital and to claim a leading part in it for himself (2Ki 22), does it not follow that Deuteronomy aimed to promote precisely this kind of sacral, institution-centered theology?

On the other side of the balance, however, stand those features of the book congenial with streams of thought in the OT that criticize the nation's leaders in general and the institution of monarchy in particular. Deuteronomy and Hosea, for example, share both a stock of theological ideas and, to an extent, the manner of their expression. This is particularly clear in their total opposition to the Baal-worship of Canaan.[33] Hosea, furthermore, was no prisoner to the kings

---

[32]For a brief explanation of the idea of a sacral Zion-tradition, see von Rad, *Old Testament Theology* (London: Oliver and Boyd, 1962), 1:44–47; see also the forthcoming volume on Zion theology in the present series.

[33]See M. Weinfeld, *Deuteronomy and the Deuteronomic School* (Oxford: Clarendon, 1972).

of his day (Hos 8:4; 10:7). Indeed, there is a strong prophetic tradition in Israel of standing up to kings when they overreached themselves or fundamentally threatened the religion of Yahweh. This tradition began at the time of Samuel, who only reluctantly permitted the institution of kingship at all in Israel, and even then both commanded and censured Saul in the name of Yahweh (1Sa 10:8; 13:7b–14; 15:16–19). It continued in Elijah, the prophet who opposed Ahab (1Ki 18:16–19). The similarities between Deuteronomy and this tradition are clear, since they evidently share a passionate concern for the government of Israel by the word of Yahweh and a hostility to all false religion (cf. Dt 7:1–5; 13:1-18, with Elijah's defeat and execution of the prophets of Baal in 1Ki 18:40).

This tradition, however, does not promote the cause of either Jerusalem or the Davidic monarchy.[34] For this reason, it has been characterized as "northern" and "covenantal" as opposed to "southern" and Davidic/Zionist.[35] The "northernness" of Deuteronomy consists, therefore, in its covenantal Yahwism, an aspect that it shares with the concerns of

[34]See, however, Hos 3:5, and F. I. Andersen and D. N. Freedman, *Hosea*, AB (New York: Doubleday, 1980), 307, for the opinion that this piece of Davidic eschatology may well be genuine. Even so, the Davidic promise is not a major theme in Hosea.

[35]The north-south distinction has been carried into the study of the prophets. Northern prophecy is said to be characterized by revelation by the "word" (Hos 1:1), whereas the southern prophets show a preference for revelation by vision (Isa 6). The former is thought, consequently, to be more congenial to covenantal theology, and the latter—because of its association with the Jerusalem temple in Isaiah—to belong in the thought world of Davidic Zionism (see D. L. Petersen, *The Roles of Israel's Prophets* [Sheffield: JSOT, 1981], 71–88; R. R. Wilson, *Prophet and Society in Ancient Israel* [Philadelphia: Fortress, 1980], 135–295. I have elsewhere criticized this line of argument, contending that there was a a single basic prophetic tradition in Israel; see my *Judgment and Promise: Interpreting the Book of Jeremiah* (Winona Lake, Ind.: Eisenbrauns/ Leicester: Inter-Varsity, 1993), ch. 8. See also W. Holladay, *Jeremiah 2*, Hermeneia (Minneapolis: Fortress, 1989), 44–53, for the influence of northern and southern prophets alike on Jeremiah.

Samuel, Elijah, and Hosea, and one that is further evidenced by the place given to Shechem in the covenantal ceremony prescribed in Deuteronomy 27:1-8.[36]

There thus appear to be two sets of features of Deuteronomy that are at odds with each other: On the one hand the centralization-law (e.g., 12:5, etc.) seems to favor the Jerusalem establishment, while on the other, the book's covenantal, prophetic spirit challenges the pretensions of all human institutions.

The apparent tension has been resolved in a number of ways. Some scholars, including von Rad, met the difficulty by arguing that the centralization-law was not a part of Urdt but a late intrusion, having originated probably in the claims of a northern sanctuary.[37] On this view, the law was understood as intending to centralize worship and thus served as an instrument of the central authorities, but was foreign to the essential spirit of Deuteronomy. By this interpretation, the book's northern, covenantal spirit is allowed to predominate.

More recent commentators, however, have found that the altar-law (a more suitable name than "centralization-law") is too deeply embedded in the language and thought of Deuteronomy to be so simply excised from it. Furthermore, they argue, it must indeed be read as referring to Jerusalem.[38] Nicholson, recognizing both northern and southern elements in Deuteronomy, is faced with the difficult question how,

---

[36]For expositions of Deuteronomy as "northern," see A. C. Welch, *The Code of Deuteronomy* (London: J. Clarke, 1924), 206-7; A. Alt, "Die Heimat des Deuteronomiums," 264-275.

[37]Von Rad, *Studies in Deuteronomy*, 67. Elsewhere he suggested that the formula of 12:5, etc., was originally at home in one of the shrines of the northern kingdom (*Deuteronomy*, OTL [London: SCM, 1966], 94). In this respect he is like Alt, who suggested Samaria after 722 B.C., now an Assyrian province, as the locale within which centralization might best be understood; "Die Heimat des Deuteronomiums," 274, n.1.

[38]Nicholson, *Deuteronomy and Tradition*, 54, 94-95; Clements, *Deuteronomy*, 81-83; also his "Deuteronomy and the Jerusalem Cult Tradition," *VT* 15 (1965), 300-12. Cf. Weinfeld, *Deuteronomic School*, 4, 55-58.

given their allegedly different ideologies, they have come to be juxtaposed. He answers that the authors of Deuteronomy were northerners who, driven south by the Assyrian invasion of their land, brought their covenantal theology with them and assimilated certain aspects of the Jerusalem traditions by way of concession. The demand for centralization was the major effect of this spirit of concession, as was the terminology of election. The process of assimilation, however, was a compromise between the different northern and southern viewpoints. Deuteronomy contained implicit criticism of the Jerusalem (or Zion) traditions and the sacral idea of kingship in particular. The resulting document, Urdt, was basically northern and covenantal in spirit, but carefully framed in the hope of acceptance by the Jerusalem authorities.[39]

Other treatments of Deuteronomy, in contrast, have argued that the book emerged more directly from Judah, building on the religious heritage of Jerusalem. O. Bächli argued that Deuteronomy was promulgated by pro-monarchical Judean circles and that, while the historical monarchy was actually criticized, a new program was set for a future Judah, based on the old institutions. In this conception, Deuteronomy's Moses actually represents the king in his roles as law-preacher, law-administrator, and highest cultic official.[40] Like Bächli, R. E. Clements believed that the book emanated from Judean circles, though these circles "demythologized" the main concepts of the Jerusalem tradition—the ark of the covenant, the sanctuary, the monarchy, and the land.[41]

The idea of demythologization was developed at some

[39]Nicholson, *Deuteronomy and Tradition*, 94–101.

[40]O. Bächli, *Israel und die Völker* (Zurich: Zwingli Verlag, 1962), 186ff. Cf. G. Mendenhall, who saw Deuteronomy as an arrangement by which political authority is preserved, while subjected to law and religious tradition ("Covenant Forms in Israelite Tradition," *BA* 17 (1954), 74.

[41]Clements, "Jerusalem Cult Tradition." Nicholson carefully distanced himself from Clements on this point; *Deuteronomy and Tradition*, 103–6.

length by M. Weinfeld. In his understanding, Deuteronomy was the work of Judeans who stood close to the court. These were not cultic officials but scribes, whose work was a literary creation based on their erudition not only in Israel's own traditions but also in the "wisdom" learning that was the common property of the ancient world. In seventh-century Judah, so Weinfeld held, this group had acquired responsibility for the propagation of the "Torah." Their radical understanding of religion led them to a thoroughgoing program of reform. They aimed at wresting the worship of Israel from the grip of the traditional priesthood and bringing it under a more enlightened control. Centralization of the cult was very much a part of this program of desacralizing religion. Their "ideal national constitution" would involve cult and priesthood as well as monarchy, judiciary, and prophecy.[42]

Weinfeld's scribes were essentially royal officials who, in providing a program for Josiah's reform, were simply furthering the tradition of royal intervention in matters of religion, a tradition that reached back to King Asa and King Jehoshaphat of Judah. The kernel, indeed, of the "Deuteronomic code" may have stemmed from those earlier reforms.[43] The scribes saw the Deuteronomic law of the king (17:14–20) as not anti-monarchic in principle, but opposed only to the Solomonic style of kingship. On the contrary, they firmly supported Josiah. Weinfeld goes further to claim that those parts of DtH that imply criticism of monarchy in general (e.g., 1Sa 8–12) are not genuinely Deuteronomic. Indeed, in the Deuteronomic view, Torah actually requires a king, or at least a "quasi-regal" figure such as Moses.[44]

At this point the interpretation of J. Halbe may be mentioned, because it contrasts sharply with those of Wein-

---

[42]Weinfeld, *Deuteronomic School*, 9, 51–58, 158–61.

[43]Ibid., 163–64.

[44]Ibid., 167–71.

feld and Bächli. While Halbe does not challenge the conventional dating of the book, he views Deuteronomy's picture of Israel as precisely one that "interrupts" the status quo. In this context, the theological significance of Moses, far from representing the Davidic monarchy, is to call Israel out of the world of monarchic state. Deuteronomy presents an ideal Israel, still on the way to being, before whom all possibilities still lie.[45] Halbe goes on to insist that the law of the king (17:14–20) is even more limiting for the king than if nothing whatever had been written about him. In it he is "rather disciplined than legitimated"; he is denied the normal basis of royal rule, and even the centralization-demand (Halbe uses the term) "by-passes him altogether."[46] Consequently, Deuteronomy is set over against world-ordering institutions, the type that he finds in Psalm 72.[47] In fact, its basic orientation and its laws—which he interprets in terms of the sociological concept of "amity"—profoundly challenge a society structured like contemporary monarchic Israel.

The question whether Deuteronomy is conservative or radical in its stance has enabled us to make similar observations to those that we made in connection with the law/grace topic. Once again, an understanding of the book's origin strongly affects the interpretation adopted. If (with Nicholson) we find that Deuteronomy is essentially northern, prophetic, and extrinsic to the Jerusalem state theology, then it must be read as a radical document, tending to disturb and undermine the status quo. If, on the other hand, we follow Weinfeld, Bächli, and others in thinking that it is genuinely southern, emanating from one class or another of state officials, then, however "reforming" its spirit, it must in some measure be seen as a program of the ruling establishment. Consequently, as with the law/grace topic, the terms of

[45]J. Halbe, "Gemeinschaft, die Welt unterbricht," in N. Lohfink, ed., *Das Deuteronomium*, 57–59.
[46]"ist 'Zentralisierung' am Koenig vorbei" (ibid., 61).
[47]Ibid., 62.

Deuteronomy have a certain impenetrability that allows the different cases to be argued more or less plausibly.

We shall argue in the next chapter that the setting of Deuteronomy is in reality much earlier than the time of Josiah, going back to a time before Israel had kings or had hardened into two divided parts. In other words, the setting before the history of the monarchy, when all possibilities remain open, is not a fiction, as in Halbe's treatment, but a reality. The anticipation of that conclusion closely affects the present discussion in three ways. First, the all-Israel range of Deuteronomy should not be conceived in terms of a conflict between "northern" and "southern" interests. Its covenantal theology is that of all Israel, and its covenantal *story* will lead in time to a monarchy in relationship with Yahweh. In this perspective, the law of the king itself anticipates something that is not yet a fact in Israel's life. Its stress is on constraint, and its aim to ensure the true primacy in Israel of Yahweh and his Torah (or law). It neither promotes nor criticizes an actual dynasty, but certainly has the potential to do the latter.

second, any human kingship in Israel is seriously qualified by Deuteronomy's theology of Yahweh's kingship. This is implicit in the structure of the book, which, as is well known, closely resembles the form of a vassal-treaty, contracted between a greater and a lesser king. In the terms of this metaphor, it is Yahweh who is the "Great King."[48] The kingship of Yahweh is further celebrated in Deuteronomy 33:5 and becomes an issue in the books of DtH—for example, in Gideon's refusal of the offer of kingship (Jdg 8:22–23) and in the responses of Samuel and Yahweh himself when the people at last do ask for a king (1Sa 8:5–8). In my view

---

[48]This lies behind the title of M. G. Kline's book on Deuteronomy, *The Treaty of the Great King* (Grand Rapids: Eerdmans, 1963). See below, ch. 3, for a discussion of the implications of the treaty-form for dating Deuteronomy.

(against Weinfeld) these parts of DtH are entirely in keeping with Deuteronomy itself.[49]

third, a pre-monarchical setting for Deuteronomy suggests that the altar-law (12:5) is not a "centralization-law." The latter idea makes sense only in a context in which claims are being entered on behalf of one existing Yahweh sanctuary over against others. The altar-law in fact opposes Yahweh's place of worship to those of *other* gods. It says nothing about the identity of the "place" that he will choose; the point is simply that *he* will choose it. Yahweh will govern in Israel's affairs, not human beings with their limited, compromised choices. This, as we shall see, is one of the great themes of the Deuteronomic corpus.

Our discussion hitherto has primarily been about methodology. We have shown how an understanding of the essence of Deuteronomy is closely bound up with concepts of origin and setting. Because the evidence in this regard is patient of different constructions, scholarship on the book has differed dramatically on fundamental matters of interpretation. Our consideration of the scholarly discussion identified two theological topics in relation to which these divergences were striking, namely, that of Law and Gospel/grace/promise and that of Deuteronomy's attitude towards the political status quo. These topics are in fact close to the heart of the concerns of Deuteronomy, as our further discussion will show.

We have, however, drawn some preliminary conclusions concerning them. First, the polarization of Law and Gospel in some treatments was unwarranted. Deuteronomy has a clear theology of the primacy of God's promise and fulfillment in the affairs of Israel, yet promise and command mesh uniquely and inextricably. second, Deuteronomy's accent on the ultimate authority of the word of Yahweh means that it will always tend to be critical of established institutions rather

---

[49]For the interpretation of the books of DtH, see below, ch. 4.

than supportive of them as such. These topics, it will be observed, are closely related to each other. Together, they amount to a theology of history in which God is sovereign and retains his freedom in relation to human beings. His life with Israel is greater than any temporary institutional arrangement, having a historical dimension that raises questions about ultimate purpose. These topics will be explored in greater depth in due course.

There remains, however, one more necessary preliminary. Our study hitherto has worked in large measure with the concept of a proto-Deuteronomy (Urdt), an original form of the book to which other material was added at a later time. We have done this in order to try to understand the terms of the scholarly debate. It will be clear by now, however, that no criteria exist for identifying either Urdt or any other allegedly supplementary material that are independent of the beliefs about setting and the theological preferences that interpreters adopt. Von Rad, for example, could justify his belief that Urdt was essentially a call to believe the promise of God by assigning the more heavily admonitory material to (unspecified) later additions.[50] Before proceeding, therefore, to a critique of some of the basic assumptions about the setting and purpose of Deuteronomy (and thence to a fuller discussion of Deuteronomic theology), it is necessary to ask what scholars mean when they distinguish between primary (Deuteronomic) and secondary (Deuteronomistic) material in Deuteronomy, and what criteria they use.

DEUTERONOMIC THEOLOGY AND THE LITERARY CRITICISM OF DEUTERONOMY

We have now seen how Deuteronomy is capable of quite different interpretations at crucial points. One influential method used to cope with its perceived polarities and

---

[50]Von Rad, *Studies in Deuteronomy*, 72.

ambiguities was literary criticism. In an earlier period of research on Deuteronomy, such criticism thought in terms of sources.[51] Modern criticism, however, takes its cue from the work of M. Noth, who thought Deuteronomy consisted of the original law-code (understood broadly according to Wellhausen), revised and expanded by an exilic "Deuteronomist"—an approach in the manner of transmission history rather than source criticism.[52] Noth believed that the Deuteronomist (Dtr) prefixed a prologue to the law-code (1:1–3:29) and made additions at the end of the book (parts of chs. 31 and 34). In these sections he believed one could find the true beginning of the narrative known as the Deuteronomistic History (DtH), for they indicate how Deuteronomy was transformed from a law-code into the introduction to that history, comprising the books of Joshua, Judges, Samuel, and Kings.[53]

Noth's thesis was an important step in formalizing the belief that different voices could be heard in Deuteronomy. While von Rad had referred rather non-specifically to "late additions" to the book that he thought were somewhat legalistic in character by comparison with the substance of the original book,[54] Noth provided a rationale for such an approach. His exilic Dtr aimed to explain the fall of Judah and Jerusalem precisely in terms of failure to keep the covenant. The final author of Deuteronomy, therefore, interpreted the covenant somewhat legalistically; to Noth, this hypothesis satisfactorily explained the presence of alleged legalistic sections in the book. The prologue, with its

---

[51]See the commentaries of F. Puukko (*Das Deuteronomium: eine literarkritische Untersuchung* [Leipzig, 1910]) and Steuernagel (*Deuteronomium und Josua*); see also F. Horst, *Das Privilegrecht Jahves*.

[52]M. Noth, *Deuteronomistic History*.

[53]M. Noth, *A History of Pentateuchal Traditions* (Englewood Cliffs, N.J.: Prentice Hall, 1972), 12–17.

[54]Von Rad, *Studies in Deuteronomy*, 72.

chronicle of Israel's lapses of faithfulness en route to the promised land, was strong evidence of this legalistic hand.

Noth's thesis proved to have more radical implications for the study of Deuteronomy than he may have foreseen. The move from source criticism to transmission history meant that the idea of an Urdt began to recede, for that idea belonged essentially to a documentary understanding of the text's origins. The old idea of a more or less clean division between an Urdt from Josiah's time and later additions[55] gave way to an idea of more gradual growth. While Noth thought in terms of a single Dtr supplementing a given Urdt, others would go on to postulate a variety of ideas within the Deuteronomistic world that were deposited in subtly differentiated layers within the corpus (i.e., both Deuteronomy and DtH). In other words, scholars shifted to a quest for "pre-Deuteronomic," "Deuteronomic," and "Deuteronomistic" material. In principle, there could be any number of editorial additions to the text. The concept became that of an inner dialogue, a debate that could go on generating itself, resulting in many "meanings" in the text—many "Deuteronomic theologies."

The attempt to describe this development of the text, of course, was not undertaken for its own sake but as a means of inquiring into Israel's religious history. It was a new stage in the search for the meaning of Deuteronomy. An example is M. Rose's aim to trace the development of the idea of exclusiveness in Yahwism. Rose recognized in principle pre-Deuteronomic material, a Deuteronomic "collection" of laws, a Deuteronomic editorial layer, and later Deuteronomistic material. He argued for the transition from a Deuteronomic "collection" to a first Deuteronomistic layer by noting a shift of focus from the exclusiveness of the people to that of the

---

[55]See, for example, Bertholet, *Deuteronomium*, HKAT (Freiburg: Mohr, 1899), XIX.

place of worship. This, he suggested, corresponded to the historical loss of the people's unity after Solomon.[56]

The question that interests us is whether this new approach offers a better hope of discovering the origin and meaning of Deuteronomy than previous attempts. In order to answer this question, it is important to have some understanding of how the method works in practice. A glance at a few works will give the flavor of this approach. S. Mittmann, for example, finds in Deuteronomy 1:1–6:3 a basic layer, supplemented in turn by two successive layers. The basic layer is essentially an itinerary, focussing on the journey from Horeb and featuring the role of the spies (1:1a, 2, 6–8, 19ff.). Its aim is simply to hold out the opportunity of obedience to a particular generation (i.e., the generation for which that layer was written).[57] The first supplementary layer provides an organizational framework for the law: a system of judges and leaders who would operate at the different levels of society (1:9–18, drawn from Ex 18 and Nu 11), and the doctrine of Holy War, advanced as the means of taking the land (Dt 3). In his view, 4:1–40 also stems largely from this layer as an elaboration of the theme of law (stressed in ch. 5).[58] The second supplementary layer expands the organizational provisions in ch. 1, the notion of "fear" (1:13–14, 17b–19), the extent of the conquest in ch. 3 (e.g., 3:1, 3–7), and certain emphases in 4:1–40. In general it has a more articulate parenetic character.[59]

Obviously this sort of treatment requires reliable criteria if it is to be convincing. One important criterion, borrowed from an early phase of Deuteronomy criticism, is that of the frequent change from singular to plural address in the book.

---

[56]M. Rose, *Der Ausschliesslichkeitsanspruch Jahwehs* (Stuttgart: Kohlhammer, 1975), 95.

[57]S. Mittman, *Deuteronomium 1:1–6:3 literarkritisch und traditionsgeschichtlich untersucht* (Berlin: de Gruyter, 1975), 164–69.

[58]Ibid., 170–74.

[59]Ibid., 174–77.

Older commentators, such as Staerk and Steuernagel, had used this phenomenon to support their source-critical attempts to isolate different "versions" of the Deuteronomic law.[60] Though its deficiencies were signaled already at that stage of the debate (e.g., by Bertholet[61]), it was given back to modern scholarship by G. Minette de Tillesse.

De Tillesse proposed that the hand of Dtr could be further discovered not just in the prologue and in the concluding sections of Deuteronomy, but also in the body of the book (5:1–30:20), in those passages in which the people were addressed not in the more normal singular but in the plural.[62] These are principally 5:1–6:1; 9:7b–10:11; 11:2–32.[63] In de Tillesse's view, these passages, some of which are quite brief (e.g., 6:14, 16, 17a; 7:4–5, 7–8a, 12a), could easily be detached from their context, leaving a text that made good sense without them. He furthermore claimed that they shared interests with the principal Deuteronomistic passages identified by Noth—above all emphasizing law, but also idolatry, land, and exile.

The number-change criterion has been accepted by several modern interpreters who, following Noth, have tried to describe the Deuteronomistic contributions to Deuteronomy. For H. D. Preuss, this phenomenon indicates the editorial process throughout chs. 5–11.[64] Others too, like

---

[60]W. Staerk, *Beiträge zur Kritik des Deuteronomiums* (Leipzig, 1894), 1–2, 97–98, 111–19; Steuernagel, *Deuteronomium und Josua*, 1st ed., IV-VI.

[61]Bertholet, *Deuteronomium*, XIX.

[62]Noth himself had made the observation that Dtr typically used the plural address. Others before him had also employed the criterion in their attempt to discover different sources underlying Deuteronomy; e.g., W. Staerk, *Beiträge zur Kritik des Deuteronomiums*; Steuernagel, *Deuteronomium*, 2d ed.

[63]G. Minette de Tillesse, "Sections 'Tu' et Sections 'Vous' dans le Deutéronome," *VT* 12 (1962), 29–87. The point is not readily appreciated in English as it is in other European languages, for, like Hebrew, they retain a distinction between singular and plural modes of address. De Tillesse's title illustrates the point.

[64]H. D. Preuss, *Deuteronomium* (Darmstadt: Wissenschaftliche Buchgesellschaft, 1982), 95, 103.

Rose, accept it in the context of a residual attachment to older literary-critical ideas, especially concerning "versions" of the altar-law in ch. 12.[65]

Clearly, however, the change from singular to plural cannot suffice as a means of distinguishing editorial layers. Mittmann, for example, thought that plural address was a characteristic of *both* the Deuteronomistic layers that he found in Deuteronomy 1:1–6:3. Obviously he needed additional criteria, as must all who are looking for multiple editorial layers (there are only two number modes!). Some, however, have rejected the use of this criterion altogether, on the grounds that the plural passages cannot be removed from their contexts without doing violence to the texts in question.[66] Changing from second singular to plural, furthermore, has been identified as a feature of rhetorical style, not only within the OT, but also beyond it.[67] Thus it can function either to arrest the hearer or to allow Israel to be conceptualized variously as a corporate body (by means of the singular) and as a collection of individuals (by means of the plural).[68] Lohfink's demonstration of the point for chs. 5–11 was followed by G. Braulik, who applied it to ch. 4, and was accepted by G. Seitz.[69] Number change, therefore, has at best become ambivalent as a criterion for distinguishing editorial

---

[65]M. Rose, *Der Ausschliesslichkeitsanspruch Jahwehs*, 95.

[66]Deut. 8:19–20 is a good example: The change occurs in the middle of a sentence, the protasis (v. 19a) using the singular and the apodosis (vv. 19b–20) adopting the plural.

[67]This has been pointed out by A. D. H. Mayes, *Deuteronomy* NCB (London: Oliphants, 1979), 35–37; K. Baltzer, *The Covenant Formulary* (Oxford: Blackwell, 1971), 33, 71. An example is the Sefire inscription 1B, lines 21–45.

[68]See N. Lohfink, *Das Hauptgebot: eine Untersuchung literarischer Einleitungsfragen zu Dtn 5–11* (Rome: Biblical Institute Press, 1963), 239ff.

[69]G. Braulik, *Die Mittel deuteronomischer Rhetorik* (Rome: Biblical Institute Press, 1978), 146–50; G. Seitz, *Redaktionsgeschichtliche Studien zum Deuteronomium* (Stuttgart: Kohlhammer, 1971), 309.

layers. Even among those who see its weakness, however, it is sometimes only reluctantly relinquished.[70]

In any case, as we have seen, number change could never stand alone as a means of identifying editorial layers. Our brief look at Mittmann revealed other criteria. His second Deuteronomistic layer, for example, was felt to be more strongly parenetic than his first. In addition, certain themes were allegedly more highly developed in one layer than another. It need hardly be said that as criteria for observing the development of a text, these are weak because of their subjectivity and could at best only supplement stronger arguments.

Scholars have sought firmer ground by resorting to a kind of argument familiar from the era of literary criticism. Deuteronomy 12 had been analysed by older literary critics into a number of sources, and newer critics also turn to it as evidence of development. Rose finds evidence of both his "collection" and subsequent redactions in that chapter.[71] In the context of this analysis, he agrees with Seitz that the centralization-formula in Deuteronomy 12ff. occurs in a longer and a shorter form (contrast 12:5 with 12:11, 21; 14:24), maintaining that these represent different redactional layers and that the shorter is more original.[72]

By way of provisional evaluation of the criticism of Deuteronomy after Noth, it may be said that it manifests considerable dependence on methods of analyzing texts that were well-known to the older literary critics. As far as the search for the true character of Deuteronomy is concerned,

---

[70]Mayes, for example, still considers that the original law-code was formulated in the singular, while the author responsible for the incorporation of Deuteronomy into the Deuteronomistic historical work used the plural (*Deuteronomy*, 37).

[71]Rose, *Der Ausschliesslichkeitsanspruch Jahwehs*, 95; cf. A. Cholewinski, *Heiligkeitsgesetz und Deuteronomium* (Rome: Biblical Institute Press, 1976), 331.

[72]Rose, *Der Ausschliesslichkeitsanspruch Jahwehs*, 97–98; Seitz, *Redaktionsgeschichtliche Studien*, 212–14.

the newer approaches have scarcely succeeded in providing securer footholds than already existed. Theories about the religious history behind the book can only be as good as the literary criticism that supports them. We shall argue that this literary criticism is far too often subjective and fragile. Furthermore, the terminology used in the newer approach (pre-Deuteronomic, Deuteronomic, Deuteronomistic) suggests that conceptions and definitions have already been imported to the task.

L. PERLITT

Before proceeding to the next chapter and a general critique of methodology used in studies on Deuteronomy, we must turn to one final interpreter in the transmission-history school, both because his work illustrates well the interdependence of literary-critical method and the reconstruction of religious history, and because it has become influential beyond the confines of the study of Deuteronomy itself.

L. Perlitt applied transmission-historical methods in his treatment of covenant theology in the OT, arguing that the full-fledged conditional covenant found in the present Deuteronomy was a late arrival in the history of Israelite religion.[73] It was, furthermore, developed through the Deuteronomistic movement, under the pressure of the events that culminated in the Exile. The process, he believed, could be traced from the pages of Deuteronomy; as was the case with earlier scholars, he brought certain theological premises to bear on the discussion, notably the idea that the theologies of promise (or grace) and law were disparate and incompatible.

In particular, Perlitt contrasted Deuteronomy 5 and 7 as exhibiting two distinct understandings of covenant theology.

---

[73]L. Perlitt, *Bundestheologie im alten Testament* (Neukirchen: Neukirchener Verlag, 1969), 1–3; beyond the influence of Noth, he explicitly relates his approach to that of Smend and Wellhausen.

Ch. 7, treated first, typifies the idea of covenant as "oath" or promise, specifically to the patriarchs. This idea he considers as the essence of the Deuteronomic covenant. It consists in the application of the theology of election, for the first time, to the people of Israel as a whole,[74] and a promise of land at a time when the land was actually under threat from Assyria (in the seventh century B.C.). Perlitt denies that the noun *bᵉriyt* must always indicate a conditional covenant in Deuteronomy. Conditional elements in ch. 7, indeed, are not original but secondary. A case in point is 7:12a (incidentally, a plural passage in the midst of singular discourse), which Perlitt argues is clearly a Deuteronomistic insertion designed to introduce a conditional note into a passage that otherwise lacks it.[75] It stands in contrast to the real view of covenant in this chapter, expressed in vv. 1–4a, 6, that the established facts of promise and blessing distinguish Israel from other nations. The specific contribution of the thinking in ch. 7 is the equation of covenant (*bᵉriyt*) and oath.[76]

Although there are secondary additions in ch. 7 that stand close to the thought of ch. 5, that chapter is, in Perlitt's view, significantly different. It includes Deuteronomy's statement of the Decalogue and was designated Deuteronomistic by Minette de Tillesse on the grounds of its plural address. Its emphasis, furthermore, is indisputably on the requirement laid upon Israel to obey God's commandments. The "covenant" (5:2), Perlitt points out, appears in this context to be virtually equated with the "decrees and laws" (v. 1) and

---

[74]Here with G. von Rad, *Das Gottesvolk*, 27–28.

[75]Perlitt, *Bundestheologie im alten Testament*, 59–60. He takes issue directly with Lohfink over this verse, who argued on structural grounds that it is integral (see *Das Hauptgebot*, 240, and cf. n. 22).

[76]This equation is itself the result of a process of thought that underlies the chapter in its present form. It is made in v. 12b, a verse that adjusts the substance of the oath to the patriarchs from land itself (as in v. 13) to covenant. This inner dialogue took place within the Deuteronomic thinking, producing the distinctive ideas of this chapter (see Perlitt, *Bundestheologie im alten Testament*, 63–64).

perhaps with the Decalogue itself[77] (compare the equation of these in 4:13). Taken by itself, ch. 5 seems to imply that keeping the commandments is the necessary precondition of enjoyment of the blessings of the land (v. 33). To Perlitt, this somewhat more legalistic conception of covenant is a conscious development from what is found in ch. 7, substituting for its association with the patriarchs a law derived from Horeb and the commands given there to the contemporary community.[78]

Through his analysis of the presence in Deuteronomy of different emphases regarding promise or grace and law, Perlitt attempts to uncover the successive stages of inner Deuteronomic dialogue. The process as he unfolds it leads to the conditionalizing of covenant by means of its connection with Horeb and finally to the legalism of Dtr, for whom obedience to the law is a precondition of blessing. He traces, in fact, a series of shifts between Deuteronomy and Dtr in relation to a variety of topics. For example, the Deuteronomic view of the law as given for blessing (6:20–25) is transformed by Dtr, who casts it into a covenantal context in which there is much greater consciousness of the curse—since Dtr already knows of the loss of land at the Exile. Thus, in a Deuteronomistic passage such as 29:23–24, the blessing is a thing of the past; now is the time of the curse. Only in a late exilic period is there relief of this misery, in a passage such as 30:1–10, one that sees the possibility of new hope even beyond the curse.[79]

Perlitt's version of the development in the Deuteronomic inner dialogue essentially turns, therefore, on the notion of the possession of the land. In fact, the loss of the land stimulates the most intense theologizing about it. This theologizing is not confined to Deuteronomy. Rather, the stream of interpretation that passes through stages known as

---

[77]Ibid., 80.
[78]Ibid., 81.
[79]Ibid., 44–45.

"Deuteronomic" and "Deuteronomistic" surfaces in other places too. An example is Genesis 15. In this connection, Perlitt argues that the tradition of the promises of the land was not originally understood covenantally; rather, that tradition comes to its culmination in its transformation into a covenant (*b'riyt*; Ge 15:18) "in a time when the simpler promissory form (J) apparently could no longer bear the weight of the contesting of the promise."[80] Thus, the story of the promise of land is re-told as a covenant story. The idea that such a promise to the patriarchs was known in the earliest traditions of Israel is an illusion. Rather, it is an impression created by a Deuteronomic retrojection, a theologumenon from the early stages of the Deuteronomic movement at the beginning of the seventh century. This fusion of promise and covenant in Genesis 15 is an attempt to secure Judah's now tenuous hold on the ancient land and serves as the prerequisite of the idea of the oath to the patriarchs in Deuteronomy 7 as a covenant.[81]

Perlitt has thus addressed issues that we saw were raised earlier by von Rad in his inquiry about the true nature of Deuteronomy. As we saw, von Rad regarded it as more a matter of promise than of law. Nicholson wanted to redress the balance by stressing the prophetic tone of the book and its anxiety about the loss of the land. Perlitt's solution is more in line with Nicholson's than with that of von Rad. In a more recent work on the development of the covenantal idea, Nicholson has acknowledged his debt to Perlitt, modifying him slightly by suggesting that the germ of the covenantal idea was already present with Hosea.[82]

Our present concern, however, has been with the *method* by which all these scholars attempt to understand the theology of Deuteronomy. Von Rad opened the discussion by

---

[80]Ibid., 75–76.

[81]Ibid., 76–77.

[82]E. W. Nicholson, *God and His People* (Oxford: Clarendon, 1986), 109–17; 179–88.

accounting for what he saw as tensions within the theology of the book and attributing them to a process of growth. He himself did not describe that process. That task was initiated by Noth, and others followed with a variety of more or less specialized treatments. Perlitt's work is the most systematic attempt to describe the growth of Deuteronomic covenant theology. Later, in another chapter, we will consider critically some of the fundamental tenets that characterize the interpretations of Deuteronomy we have been examining.

◆ 3 ◆

Dating Deuteronomy

The attempt to articulate the theology of Deuteronomy is, as we have now seen, complicated by the elusiveness of certain interconnecting questions. The view taken of its precise date and setting affects the assessment of its character and purpose. Historical, literary, and theological questions are indissolubly linked. The literary-critical separation of "grace"-discourse and "law"-discourse into different strands, for example, is part of a historical-critical argument that the final form of Deuteronomy emerges from a time of crisis and loss. An evaluation of the points of view already examined, therefore, must in the end treat historical considerations and literary ones together. We begin, however, with some attention to the historical question.

THE ISSUE OF DATING

What follows cannot be an exhaustive treatment of the date of Deuteronomy, but rather a consideration of some of the factors involved. We noted in the previous chapter that the close connection once supposed between Deuteronomy and the reform of King Josiah is no longer taken for granted;

yet the connection with the seventh century has largely been retained. It is time to consider more closely the strength of the arguments for this continued association. If Deuteronomy is not an instrument of Josiah's reform, what precisely binds it to the seventh century? We shall consider a number of criteria used in dating the book.

(1) Land

Some scholars have approached the dating of Deuteronomy by means of its characteristic features. We have seen how the theology of land played a part in the argument that this book belonged in the seventh century, for that was the time when its tenure became precarious. Perlitt, for example, distinguishes between an early (pre-Yahwistic) tradition of land-promise and a later development of that tradition. The former he found in Genesis 12:7a, which reflects the confidence of the Davidic age (the age of victory) and needed no theological elaboration.[1] Genesis 15, in contrast, contains a repetition of the land-promise, a promise that Perlitt sees as superfluous to the narrative recorded there. He follows a long tradition of interpretation that sees in the theological expansiveness of this chapter a reflection of a less secure age.[2] The transformation of the simple promise (12:7a) into a "covenant" (15:18) can be traced to a period of theological creativity between the Elohistic document (eighth century) and Deuteronomy; this period is the essential foreground of Deuteronomy 7.[3] This theologizing was characterized by an

[1]L. Perlitt, *Bundestheologie im alten Testament* (Neukirchen: Neukirchener Verlag, 1969), 67–68.

[2]Perlitt cites Gunkel: "The piece must come from a time in which the possession of the land began to be in doubt for Israel" (*Genesis* [Göttingen: Vandenhoeck and Ruprecht, 1902], 167). Cf. J. Hoftijzer, *Die Verheissungen an die drei Erzvaeter*, Leiden: Brill, 1956), 99; Lohfink, *Das Landverheissung als Eid* (Stuttgart: Katholisches Bibelwerk, 1987), 32–33; G. von Rad, *Genesis: A Commentary*, OTL (Philadelphia: Westminster, 1973), 190.

[3]Perlitt, *Bundestheologie im alten Testament*, 71–77.

understanding of history in terms of covenant and enabled Deuteronomy 7 to think of the commitment to the fathers not simply as a promise, but as a *covenantal oath*.

These arguments, however, produce no hard evidence for a date in the seventh century. Rather, they rely heavily on the thinking of the documentary hypothesis (into which Gen 15 did not easily fit)[4] and on the unsubstantiated claim that a theologically sophisticated promise of land can only date from a time of threat to it. Even granted such a thesis, the choice of the seventh century is not compelling, since apart from the immediate time of David and Solomon, the land was more or less under threat in almost every period before and after. The theology of land alone cannot pinpoint Deuteronomy to the seventh century. In reality, other factors govern the belief that it does so, not least of which is the mere weight of the scholarly tradition that Deuteronomy is a seventh-century Judean document.

(2) Brotherhood

Similar points may be made about the theology of brotherhood. Seen against a seventh-century background, such an idea is comprehensible as a nostalgia in an age of repressive centralization for the tribal structure that had nourished the old religion.[5] Yet the need for this idea of Israel as a brotherhood might have just as easily been felt in the time of Solomon—or even of David himself, since one effect of David's thrust towards political unity in Israel was to expose starkly the fissures that even then threatened to be incurable (2Sa 3–4; 15–18; 20).

[4]C. Westermann, *Genesis 12–36* (London: SPCK/ Minneapolis: Augsburg, 1985), 214.

[5]See G. von Rad, *Das Gottesvolk* (Stuttgart: Kohlhammer, 1929), 50.

(3) Anti-Canaanite Polemic

In the previous chapter we referred to the debate over Deuteronomy's relationship to the Jerusalem cult. That debate, we argued, had reached an impasse because of the failure of scholars to agree on the fundamental question how far the book favored it. What is certain, however, is that Deuteronomy evinces marked hostility to Canaanite religion. This is clear both in the "framework" (Dt 1–11; 27ff.) and in the law-code. Chapter 7, for example, sets the divine election of Israel in the context of a rejection of the existing nations in the land, because of the danger that Israel might be led astray by their worship. Similarly, within the law-code, the command to worship at "the place the LORD your God will choose" is accompanied by the requirement to destroy the "places" of Canaanite worship (12:1–5). In my view, what is sometimes understood as Deuteronomy's hostility to cultic religion is no such thing, but an insistence on the worship of Yahweh alone at the expense of other gods.[6] The idea that Deuteronomy is anti-cultic cannot be justified exegetically, but only in the context of an approach that sees it, on other grounds, as an attempt to come to terms with the loss of temple and land and with the germ of a religion of Torah that could survive such losses.[7]

The question, then, is at what period of Israel's history is such opposition to Canaanite worship likely to have had so high a profile? Various answers have been given. Least plausible, it seems to me, are those that date Deuteronomy as late as the exile. Dating the book as late as this requires that the anti-Canaanite material be regarded as somewhat theo-

---

[6]Thus against Weinfeld's understanding, as outlined in chapter 2. See further J. Milgrom's review of Weinfeld's *Deuteronomy and the Deuteronomic School*, *Israel Exploration Journal* 23 (1973), 156–61, for his view that Deuteronomy has a positive view of cultic religion.

[7]See, for example, Noth, *The Deuteronomistic History* (Sheffield: JSOT, 1981), 92–95; Weinfeld, *Deuteronomy and the Deuteronomic School* (Oxford: Clarendon, 1972), 44–45.

retical in nature.[8] Yet there is no good reason to think that Deuteronomy has such a theoretical character. There were serious dangers to Judah's Yahwism in the peri-exilic period in the shape of both formalism and syncretism, as the book of Jeremiah testifies (Jer 7:1–15; 44). Yet Deuteronomy's view of the dangers to Yahwism seems far removed from Jeremiah's; as a warning against contemporary threats to true religion it would be curiously oblique. Nothing in Deuteronomy, in fact, compares with the frequent prophetic criticism of debased worship. (In this respect Jeremiah is in a long tradition; cf. Am 5:21–24; Micah 6:6–8; Isa 1). Its analysis of the dangers to Israel is in terms neither of formalism nor, directly, of syncretism, but rather of the stark choice between Yahweh and other gods.

Deuteronomy's antagonism to false religion differs both from that of the prophets in general and from that of DtH. It is thus different at a crucial point from two books with which it otherwise has much in common, namely Jeremiah and Kings. Both the prophets and DtH are characterized, in their criticism of Israel's and Judah's apostasies, by an approach that is generally unfavorable to kingship. This is not kingship in a theoretical sense, but in the context of a living experience of the Davidic dynastic monarchy and the succession of northern royal houses. Hosea, for example, trumpets his disillusionment with kingship as he knew it (Hos 10:3), and Jeremiah writes finis to the historic Davidic dynasty (Jer 22). In 1, 2 Kings, furthermore, the crux of the life of Israel and Judah before God is the way in which the kings had been behaving in respect of the non-Yahwistic places of worship. Their failure in this regard ensured the fall of both kingdoms.[9]

---

[8]G. Hoelscher, "Komposition und Ursprung des Deuteronomiums," *ZAW* 40 (1922), 161–255; cf. Alt, "Die Heimat des Deuteronomiums," in *Kleine Schriften zur Geschichte des Volkes Israel* (Munich: C. H. Beck'sche Verlagsbuchhandlung, 1953), 2:262.

[9]On the theology of 1, 2 Kings, see McConville, "Narrative and Meaning in the Books of Kings," *Biblica* 70 (1989), 31–49.

If, on the other hand, Deuteronomy is theoretical anywhere, it is in relation to the king. The law of 17:14–20 does have the character of a prospective program rather than an urgent opposition to contemporary crimes. It differs noticeably from 1, 2 Kings, moreover, in its conception of royal misdemeanour, avoiding the idea of the king as chiefly responsible for the right conduct of the cult, requiring instead his honoring of his fellow-Israelites in submission to the law, and deprecating his pursuit of personal wealth.

In relation to the pre-exilic prophets, the conception of the king's faults is distinctive. Kings are upbraided by prophets for a variety of offences. Hosea has in mind the northern kings' failures in the area of cult (Hos 10:3; cf. 7:6, with its probable allusion to the golden calf of Jeroboam I; Hosea is close in this respect to 1, 2 Kings). Isaiah rebukes Ahaz for his failure to trust Yahweh and his recourse instead to a political alliance (Isa 7:3–9). Neither of these concerns is specifically connected with kingship in Deuteronomy. In the case of Jeremiah, the accusation against kings is the general one of self-aggrandizement and neglect of the leader's proper duties (Jer 22:13–17; 23:1–2). Even here, the terms are not those of Deuteronomy (i.e., no "brotherhood" or Torah-keeping), and, of course, Jeremiah names particular kings. (So also, incidentally, is Josiah named, whose righteousness is acknowledged, though scarcely acclaimed; 22:15b–16).

Deuteronomy comes closest to a prophetic view of Israel's history in ch. 32. Here, instead of the more typical Deuteronomic warning against future apostasy, the perspective is rather that of a present fact (see vv. 15–18). In its terminology, furthermore, it is sometimes reminiscent of the prophets (e.g., compare Dt 32:10–18 with Jer 2; Dt 32:17 with Jer 2:11; Dt 32:21 with Hos 1:9; Dt 32:19 with Isa 1:1; Dt 32:28–29 with Isa 1:3; Dt 32:23–25 with Jer 21:9; Dt 32:39a with Isa 40:18, 25; 41:4; 43:25a; Dt 32:29 with Hos 6:1). Even here, however, Deuteronomy lacks the prophetic critique of kingship. The Song of Moses presupposes a period in the land within which there has been some defection to idolatrous religion. Yet beyond this, it affords little evidence for specific dating.[10]

It follows, therefore, that Deuteronomy's position on cultic worship does not help to locate the book at any particular date in the monarchy. Its view is so distinct from the types of criticism of cult and kings that are found in the prophets—who clearly do react to specific conditions—that it is impossible to say with confidence on these grounds that Deuteronomy belongs just before or during the exile.

In regard to anti-Canaanitism, however, Deuteronomy's position is comprehensible as soon as there is a Yahwistic Israel in Canaan. This was the view of Welch (though it has to be stated in slightly different terms from his in order to acknowledge developments in the study of Israel's history),[11] and it is still preferable to that of Hoelscher. Deuteronomy, though distinct from the prophets in its warnings about false religion, is nevertheless too passionate to be merely theoretical.[12]

(4) The Laws

The question of dating has also been approached in connection with the laws. In general, of course, the laws legislate for the time when Israel is already established in the

---

[10]The Song of Moses has often been dated very early in Israel's history (e.g., by Eissfeldt and Albright); see P. C. Craigie, *The Book of Deuteronomy*, NICOT (Grand Rapids: Eerdmans, 1976), 374, for bibliography. Craigie notes the difficulty in finding secure points of contact with events in Israel's history. For links between the Song and prophecy, see G. E. Wright, "The Lawsuit of God," in B. W. Anderson and W. Harrelson, eds., *Israel's Prophetic Heritage* (New York: Harper Brothers, 1962), 26–67. Wright sees the typical prophetic lawsuit pattern in Dt 32.

[11]A. C. Welch, *The Code of Deuteronomy* (London: J. Clarke, 1924), 51. The question of the origins of Israel in the land is thus raised. See J. J. Bimson, "The Origins of Israel in Canaan: An Examination of Recent Theories," *Themelios* 15 (1989), 4–15, for an account and critique of recent trends.

[12]See note 8.

land. An example is Deuteronomy 21:9, the law of the unsolved homicide, in which the requisite measures are taken by the elders of nearby cities. Both agricultural and city life are taken for granted everywhere (e.g. 22:6–11). In this respect, Deuteronomy is no different from the Book of the Covenant, which had also made such assumptions (e.g., Ex 22:5–8). Leaving aside the question whether both codes might in fact legislate for life in the land in an anticipatory way, there is certainly no evidence as yet for a particular period in Israel's existence there.

More interestingly, we have already noted that early in the criticism of Deuteronomy, the laws of this book varied considerably in their details from laws on similar subjects in other codes. They not only manifested strong similarities with the laws in the Book of the Covenant (Ex 20–23), but they appeared to expand upon them, introducing their own typical emphases. Thus, for example, the law of slave-release (Dt 15:12–18; cf. Ex 21:2–6) strongly develops both the idea of the brotherhood of all Israelites and that of the land as the gift of God, and it becomes the model for Israel's ethics. It is not surprising that similar arguments to those we have already observed in relation to the book in general appear again in connection with the laws (see above on brotherhood and land).

A special class of laws, however, that features prominently in the present argument is one that bears upon sacrifice and worship. These laws exhibit noticeable differences from cultic laws in other books of the Pentateuch. For example, Deuteronomy's law of the tithe (14:22–29) appears as a feast for all Israelites, whereas in Numbers 18:20–25 it had the character of a tax for the benefit of the Levite. Early critics saw such differences as irreconcilable conflict and explained them in terms of separate origins of the law-codes.[13]

---

[13]S. R. Driver, *A Critical and Exegetical Commentary on Deuteronomy*, ICC (Edinburgh: T. and T. Clark, 1895), 169.

There is, furthermore, a certain tendency in the cultic laws. They are not laws in any pure or abstract sense; rather, they exhibit in their expression, with some consistency, the dominant theological themes of the book.[14] To observe this, of course, merely throws us back to the question at issue, namely, in what circumstances did the book actually arise?

One feature of the cultic laws, however, has widely been thought to offer an answer to this very question: the altar-law itself, i.e., the requirement that Israel should bring their sacrificial offerings to "the place the LORD your God will choose . . . to put his Name there for his dwelling" (e.g., 12:5). We have already given some attention to the meaning of this requirement.[15] Our present concern is more narrowly with its role in dating the book.

Early critical studies of Deuteronomy took the altar-law as evidence of its emanation from the movement that lay behind the reform of Josiah. The command, apparently more limiting in respect of the place of legitimate sacrifice than Exodus 20:24-25, was regarded as a veiled program for precisely those measures that Josiah actually took according to the account in 2 Kings 22-23.[16] Certain literary-critical treatments of Deuteronomy, furthermore, proposed several layers of material judged by the criterion of immediacy of relationship to the reform.[17]

Even the altar-law, however, has failed in subsequent enquiry to fasten Deuteronomy irrevocably to the reign of Josiah. This is so for at least two reasons. First, there is the question of its meaning. Ever since the work of A. C. Welch, the argument has been canvassed that Deuteronomy's altar-law does not in fact require centralization. He pointed out

---

[14]This is the main thesis of my *Law and Theology in Deuteronomy* (Sheffield: JSOT, 1984).

[15]See chapter 2, above.

[16]Driver, *Deuteronomy*, 136-38.

[17]For example, F. Horst, *Das Privilegrecht Jahves* (Göttingen: Vandenhoeck and Ruprecht, 1930), 1ff.

that the phrase that is often translated "in one of your tribes" (e.g., 12:14) may also be rendered "in any of your tribes"; therefore, the typical terminology of the law does not after all aim to legitimate worship at one sanctuary only. Though Welch made an exception for 12:5, thinking it demanded exclusive rights for one place, it is arguable nevertheless that Deuteronomy is less interested in the number of legitimate places than in their dedication to Yahweh rather than to the gods of the other nations.[18]

second, it has been argued that the altar-law has its own history of transmission. That is, while the author of Kings clearly understood it to apply to Jerusalem in the time of Josiah—indeed, from the time of the building of the temple (see 1Ki 3:2; 2Ki 21:4)—the formula may have been understood to apply to other places at other times.[19] The historical-critical background to this theory used to be the now unfashionable belief of M. Noth that Israel was organized in the pre-monarchical period as an amphictyony, according to Greek analogies, in which tribes were united by a central shrine.[20] The amphictyony theory aside, however, the OT contains evidence that the formula known from the altar-law of Deuteronomy was *not* understood only of Jerusalem. Most telling is Jeremiah 7:12–15, an argument that rests on the identification of Shiloh as the place "where I first made a dwelling for my Name." Jeremiah here draws on the

---

[18]Welch, *The Code of Deuteronomy*; cf. G. J. Wenham, "Deuteronomy and the Central Sanctuary" (*TB* 22 [1971], 113-18), who argues that Deuteronomy merely requires a central sanctuary, while it tolerates other lesser ones; also McConville, *Law and Theology*, for the argument that the real issue in the altar-law is that of Yahweh's choice.

[19]F. Dumermuth, "Zur deuteronomischen Kulttheologie und ihren Voraussetzungen," *ZAW* 70 (1958), 59–98; von Rad, *Deuteronomy*, OTL (London: SCM, 1966), 94; Alt, "Die Heimat des Deuteronomiums," 274, n. 1. See also ch. 2 above, n. 37.

[20]M. Noth, *Das System der zwölf Stämme Israels* (Stuttgart: Kohlhammer, 1930). See the criticisms of A. D. H. Mayes, *Israel in the Period of the Judges* (London: SCM, 1974), and O. Bächli, *Amphiktyonie im alten Testament* (Basel: Friedrich Reinhardt Verlag, 1977).

Samuel narratives, in which Shiloh appears as a sanctuary for all Israel (1Sa 1–3). What is significant is that those narratives occur within DtH, and Jeremiah too, especially in sermonic material such as is found in Jeremiah 7:1–15, has evident affinities with Deuteronomy. Accordingly, a view is found in material acknowledged to be related to Deuteronomy that Yahweh's chosen place was not always Jerusalem, but that Jerusalem merely succeeded in time to that honor.

In modern treatments of Deuteronomy, as we have seen, von Rad's idea that the altar-law constituted a separate strand has rightly been found unconvincing. The altar-law fits too well with the interests of the rest of the book. R. E. Clements, for example, stresses this integrity of the altar-law in the context of his belief that Deuteronomy derives essentially from the late seventh century. For him, the "place" is undoubtedly Jerusalem.[21] Yet the argument about the integrity of the altar-law cuts both ways. If, in contrast to Clements' view, it is taken to be a memory of real conditions in pre-monarchic Israel, then its coherence with the themes of Deuteronomy may instead have the effect of allowing much more of the book to be dated earlier than the seventh century.

(5) Style

Another feature of Deuteronomy that has often been used in the attempt to date it is its style. Unquestionably, the book's style is one of its distinctive characteristics.[22] It has affinities with parts of both Jeremiah and 1, 2 Kings, leading to the common supposition that the style in question is typical of the seventh century.[23] Some, indeed, go further and claim

---

[21]R. E. Clements, *Deuteronomy* OT Guides [Sheffield: JSOT, 1989], 28.

[22]See S. R. Driver, *Deuteronomy*, lxxvii–lxxxviii.

[23]E. Janssen, *Juda in der Exilszeit: Ein Beitrag zur Frage der Entstehung des Judentums* (Göttingen: Vandenhoeck and Ruprecht, 1956), 105–107; E. W. Nicholson, *Preaching to the Exiles: A Study of the Prose Tradition in the Book of*

that style is the only reliable criterion for the identification of a Deuteronomic or Deuteronomistic hand in a piece of writing.[24]

The similarities between Deuteronomy, Jeremiah, and Kings are not to be denied. They can, however, be exaggerated, and their significance is not easy to evaluate. In the case of Jeremiah, the so-called prose sections of that book—the ones that most closely resemble the style of Deuteronomy—exhibit a large number of characteristics that are not found in the latter book but may be regarded as distinctively Jeremianic.[25] More importantly, the argument from style is no longer widely thought to be as cogent as it once was.[26] The similarities between Deuteronomy and other books are in reality capable of various interpretations. Furthermore, style cannot in principle be a decisive guide to dating in isolation from considerations of content and meaning.

These observations tend to confirm what we have already seen in the previous chapter, namely, that the tendency to date Deuteronomy in the seventh century owes

Jeremiah (Oxford: Blackwell, 1970), 39–57; M. Weinfeld, _Deuteronomy and the Deuteronomic School_, 10–58.

[24]See, for example, T. Veijola, _Das Königtum in der Beurteilung der deuteronomistischen Historiographie_ (Helsinki: Suomalainen Tiedeakatemia, 1977), 13.

[25]See J. Bright, "The Date of the Prose Sermons of Jeremiah," _JBL_ 70 (1951), 15–35; H. Weippert, _Die Prosareden des Jeremiabuches_ (Berlin: de Gruyter, 1973).

[26]W. McKane's trenchant criticism of Thiel's work on Jeremiah in this respect shows how far the criterion of style was capable of being overpressed, and indeed used in a double-edged way; see McKane, "Relations Between Poetry and Prose in the Book of Jeremiah with Special Reference to Jeremiah III 6–11 and XII 14–17," _SVT_ 32 (1980), 224. Notice also J. L. Kugel's strictures about assumptions made in OT studies about the distinctions between prose and poetry in _The Idea of Biblical Poetry_ (New Haven, CT: Yale Univ. Press, 1981), 69–87. See my own discussions of the style criterion in _Judgment and Promise: Interpreting the Book of Jeremiah_ (Winona Lake, Ind.: Eisenbrauns/Leicester: Inter-Varsity, 1993) and in "1 Kings VIII 46–53 and the Deuteronomic Hope," _VT_ 42 (1992), 67–79.

much to habit; the data themselves are capable of quite other constructions.

(6) Form

Closely related to the style of the book is its form. Discussions of the form of Deuteronomy bear directly on the question of both its dating and its interpretation.

In the previous chapter, we saw the tendency for theological conceptions of Deuteronomy (such as von Rad's) to go hand in hand with beliefs about its composition. Noth's theory of an exilic Deuteronomistic edition of Deuteronomy established in practice an indissoluble link between evaluations of theology and of literary form. Thus Minette de Tillesse tried to show a correspondence between plural address and legalistic theology, while Perlitt attempted systematically to distinguish redactional layers in the book on the basis of different understandings of "covenant." In order to place these approaches to Deuteronomy in perspective, it is necessary to consider the question of form more widely.

As is well known, one of the major factors in the criticism of Deuteronomy in the present century has been the discovery of formal similarities between it and certain Ancient Near Eastern treaties and law-codes. Mendenhall's initial observation of parallels between Hittite vassal-treaties of the second millennium B.C. and parts of the OT was extended to Deuteronomy by conservative scholars, notably Kitchen and Kline. They argued that this proximity of form was evidence that, like the treaties in question, Deuteronomy must have originated in the second millennium, especially since that specific form is not attested elsewhere after the late second millennium and a sudden reappearance of the form after a lacuna of several centuries is inexplicable.[27] It followed that

---

[27]K. A. Kitchen, *Ancient Orient and the Old Testament* (London: Tyndale Press, 1966), 90–102; M. G. Kline, *The Treaty of the Great King* (Grand

the early date of Deuteronomy was the simplest and most cogent explanation of the facts.

The argument, however, has not gone uncriticized. It has been questioned, for example, at the level of the interpretation of the data. Weinfeld argued that first-millennium Assyrian treaties resembled Deuteronomy more closely than the Hittite treaties did. He also pointed out that Deuteronomy bore certain features of ancient Near Eastern law-codes as well as of treaties. Furthermore, the marks of the treaty-form on Deuteronomy were to be explained not by the supposition that the book actually functioned as a treaty, but rather came as a result of literary influence, in the context of that scribal erudition to which, as we have seen, he believed the production of the book was due. McCarthy, too, maintained that the treaty-form was an idea that informed the various stages of the book's growth, but that the form first made an impact on Israel's religion in Josiah's reform. This kind of approach has had further support from Nicholson, who has argued that covenantal forms in OT literature represent essentially a theological idea, one that enters Israel's thinking at a relatively late date.[28]

It is true that Deuteronomy does not perfectly resemble any one kind of ancient treaty or law-code. However, the choice of these forms is no accident. Deuteronomy resembles treaty and law, not just in style, but also in substance. To say

Rapids: Eerdmans, 1963). Cf. G. E. Mendenhall, "Covenant Forms in Israelite Tradition," *BA* 17 (1954), 50–76. Mendenhall himself did not make the connection with Deuteronomy, applying his insight only to the Decalogue and Jos 24.

[28]Weinfeld, *Deuteronomy and the Deuteronomic School*, 65–69; 146–57; for the literary nature of the composition of Deuteronomy, see especially 150–51, 157. See also D. J. McCarthy, *Treaty and Covenant*, 2d ed. (Rome: Pontifical Biblical Institute, 1978), 157ff.; Nicholson, *God and his People* (Oxford: Clarendon, 1986). Not all conservative scholars, incidentally, agree that Deuteronomy's closest formal links are with the Hittite treaties; see D. J. Wiseman, *The Vassal Treaties of Esarhaddon* (London: British School of Archaeology in Iraq, 1958), 28.

that the use of the form of a covenant (or treaty) is merely a theological idea does not do full justice to the nature of that idea. Deuteronomy presents itself as a binding document upon Israel. Its laws were to be written on plaster-covered stones in a solemn ceremony (Dt 27:2–3), and as far as we can tell, were meant to be kept.[29] Like a treaty, furthermore, the book was to be deposited in the nation's main sanctuary (31:26). While there is a sense in which the idea of Yahweh as the "Great King" in the terminology of the vassal-treaty is "metaphorical," nevertheless it was intended to have practical reality. As long as Israel truly recognized the kingship of Yahweh, no other king would lord it over them. The covenant with Yahweh had a hard political aspect.

For these reasons, I think that those treatments of the book that posit a cultic background have done most justice to its nature as a covenant-document.[30] Deuteronomy does not make sense unless it aims in reality to govern the whole life of Israel, and this aim must be sanctioned by its solemn acceptance at the heart of Israel's life—its worship. We have noted that McCarthy, like Nicholson, thought of Deuteronomy primarily as a theological idea. However, he evidently hesitated at this point, for he also said that the book participated somehow in the *genre* of treaty. Given the form in which it is couched, it is hard to see how it could do otherwise.[31]

A. D. H. Mayes, in a relatively recent commentary, has returned to the idea that Deuteronomy most closely resem-

---

[29]The prophets appear to assume that they were intended to be kept; Am 2:8 could be based on Dt 24:12–13 (though cf. Ex 22:26–27).

[30]We have noticed chiefly the treatment of von Rad. Mention may also be made in this connection of Lohfink's theory that the "Book of the Law," discovered in Josiah's reform, was the ancient covenant document of Jerusalem, having a pre-history going back to the time of the tribal league and having been the inspiration for the various covenant renewals or reforms that were instigated by the kings of Judah; see "Die Bundesurkunde des Königs Josias," *Biblica* 44 (1963), 461ff.

[31]McCarthy, *Treaty and Covenant*, 175–76. Cf. n. 29, above.

bles the Hittite treaties, though he thinks that that form came to be superimposed on Deuteronomy only at the time of the exile. It is questionable, however, whether his idea of a "treaty-tradition," explaining the late assimilation of the idea to Deuteronomy, has been demonstrated.[32] In my view, it makes more sense to suppose that the form of the book is ancient, and that it was preserved in the worship of Israel because of its association with the Ark of the Covenant.

There is a further fundamental point: No amount of formal arguments can by themselves compel a conclusion about dating or composition. Rather, they must be accompanied by arguments about content. If Deuteronomy demonstrably contains features that date it to the seventh century or to the exile, then its formal similarities to Hittite treaties will be highly fragile as an argument for its early dating. This point has been well made by R. E. Clements, who believes that the book can indeed be dated to the seventh century, for the kinds of reasons to which we have paid attention above.[33] I have argued, however, that those grounds are not in fact as strong as Clements and others think, because the data are, at best, capable of diverse interpretations. Indeed, in the case of Deuteronomy's hostility to Canaanite religion, we thought it consistent with a date at least as early as the beginning of the monarchy. I have argued elsewhere that the content of Deuteronomy in general favors such a view.[34]

Some scholars, however, deny in principle that formal analogies from the Ancient Near East might be relevant to an understanding of the origin and composition of Deuteronomy. H. D. Preuss clearly believes that the arguments of Kline, Craigie, and others simply cut a Gordian knot; their comparisons assume a unity of the book that ought to be established

---

[32]Mayes, *Deuteronomy*, NCB (London: Oliphants, 1979), 33, 54.

[33]Clements, *Deuteronomy*, 69–76.

[34]See my *Law and Theology*. This is in spite of Clements' statement (*Deuteronomy*, 20) that my argument is a formal one that pays no attention to content; the case is almost the reverse.

on independent grounds before making comparisons with other literature.[35] But this is merely dogmatic. Modern studies of many OT books are showing that the texts have a coherence that was undreamt of in the heyday of the older methods. And such coherence, where it exists, cannot be dismissed as in principle irrelevant to the historical-critical task. If arguments based on alleged incoherence in a text are supposed to be able to yield historical-critical or religio-historical results, the reverse must also be true. On this issue, Perlitt is entirely in line with Preuss. The contradiction he postulates between covenant as oath and covenant as command pre-empts an enquiry into the structure of individual chapters or of wider sections of the book. In my view, in contrast, a formal enquiry might invalidate his premise.

In fact, Deuteronomy has a kind of inner unity that the treaty-analogy merely begins to suggest. As I have shown elsewhere, a sustained mirror-image relationship exists between one of the dominant thrusts of chs. 1–11 (Yahweh's leading or bringing of Israel to the promised land) and the consistent demand in the cultic laws in chs. 12–26 (that Israelites respond in worship). This relationship can be described in terms of specific terminology: a correspondence between Yahweh *bringing* Israel to a *place* and Israel *bringing* offerings to a *place*; between Yahweh acting *before* Israel and Israel worshiping *before* Yahweh; between Yahweh *giving* the land and other good things and Israel *giving*, in imitation of him, to the needy.[36] The distribution of these features strongly suggests an intentional symmetry of thought in which Yahweh's grace is met appropriately by a response of Israel in obedience and worship. These observations show that law and grace, rather than being rival views, mesh neatly in

---

[35]H. D. Preuss, *Deuteronomium* (Darmstadt: Wissenschaftliche Buchgesellschaft, 1982), 66–67.

[36]I have elaborated this argument in *Law and Theology*, 33–36.

Deuteronomy; consequently, to allege a contrast between them cannot be useful for religio-historical reconstruction.

The line of thought may be pursued in relation to Deuteronomy 7, crucial to Perlitt's thesis. He believed that this chapter aimed to equate covenant and patriarchal oath. Therefore, elements perceiving it otherwise (e.g., vv. 9–10, 12a) could not be original. There are, however, objections to this view. First, the deletion of v. 12a is unwarranted and merely an exigency of Perlitt's theory.[37] The same is true of the belief that vv. 9–10 are not original in the context. In fact, that strong statement of mutual obligation in covenant is an essential part of the message of the chapter. That this is so is demonstrated by an extended analogy between the form of ch. 7 and that of ch. 12. Both chapters form an ABB'A' pattern, according to the following format:

A.   7:1–5   The promise of God in giving and hold-
                    ing the land
  B.   7:6–11   Holiness of God's chosen people
  B'. 7:12–16   The blessing of the land as the cor-
                    ollary of the people's holiness
A'. 7:17-26   The promise of God in giving and hold-
                    ing the land

A.   12:1–4   The promise of God in giving and hold-
                    ing the land
  B.   12:5–12   Holiness of the people expressed in
                    the command to worship at the
                    place God chooses
  B'. 12:13–28   The blessing of the land as the cor-
                    ollary of the people's holiness
A'. 12:29–13:1   The promise of God in giving and hold-
                    ing the land

---

[37]Perlitt, *Bundestheologie im alten Testament*, 61; for contrast, see N. Lohfink, *Das Hauptgebot: eine Untersuchung literarischer Einleitungsfragen zu Dtn 5–11* (Rome: Biblical Institute Press, 1963), 240–41.

Chapters 7 and 12 are both framed by paragraphs that stress the promise of God in giving the land and in ensuring Israel's holding of it in the face of opposition from other nations (A 7:1–5; A' 7:17–26; cf. A 12:1–4; A' 12:29–13:1). These already contain command as well as promise, for the two ideas are virtually inseparable in Deuteronomy. More interesting is the way in which the B and B' sections relate to each other. These both reflect on the holiness of Israel: 7:6–11 (B) relates that holiness to God's choice of his people, whereas 12:5–12 expresses the holiness in the command to worship at the place that God will choose. In the B' sections (7:12–16; 12:13–28), the blessing of the land is the corollary of the people's holiness.

The two chapters are not, of course, identical; rather there is a progression between them that is expressed in the implications of holiness: in ch. 7 holiness is covenant faithfulness generally (7:9–10); in ch. 12, holiness is a proper response in worship. This progression belongs to the correspondences that exist between the larger sections of the book.[38] In ch. 7, therefore, an understanding of the wider context makes Perlitt's view of 7:12 the more arbitrary.

The purpose of the foregoing argument has been to illustrate the lines that a study of the relationship between form and content in Deuteronomy might take. The practical consequence of an approach like this, in contrast to that of Perlitt and many other scholars, is to show once again that the theology of the book becomes more subtle in its analysis. For Perlitt and the others, law and grace are alternative propositions on a historical time-line that throws up different attempted solutions to the problem of Israel's identity and their relationship with God. On the approach advocated here, however, Deuteronomy (as regards the topic of law and grace) is a sophisticated theological reflection. It will be our task to attempt to understand this kind of reflection more carefully. My point here has been to try to show that there are dimensions to the attempt, especially in the relationship

---

[38] I have shown this at length in my *Law and Theology*, 33–36, 58–67.

between form and content, that many scholars do not recognize, and that therefore many arguments and assumptions about the date and origin of the book are weak.

CONCLUSIONS FOR
DEUTERONOMIC THEOLOGY

Our purpose in the present chapter has been to evaluate critically the historical-critical arguments upon which interpretations of Deuteronomy, and hence of "Deuteronomic Theology," have been built. Our study has led us to certain interim conclusions about the nature of that theology by showing the difficulty of discovering it by means of the literary- and historical-critical arguments so often deployed. Scholars have made far too many assumptions about the nature and setting of the literature, namely, that it grew in the context of a movement that began in the seventh century and continued into and beyond the exile; close examination shows such assumptions are unjustifiable. We saw in the previous chapter, furthermore, that fundamental aspects of the interpretation of Deuteronomy depended largely on literary- and historical-critical decisions. Two major issues were raised in that chapter. The first one was the question whether the note of warning (or "law") predominated in the basic theological orientation of the book, or whether that of promise (or "grace") did so. Our study has shown that the question is misconceived, for in fact the notes of promise and warning are subtly interwoven—two poles of a single message. A consequence is that any quest for the "true" setting of the "original" book (Urdt) in terms of one or other of these poles is abortive.

The second issue concerned whether Deuteronomy was favorable to, or critical of, the institutions of monarchy and cult. We have already suggested that Deuteronomy is by no means a pillar of the institutional status quo. When we consider Deuteronomy as a coherent statement, this opinion gains further support.

◆ 4 ◆

The Deuteronomic Idea
in Joshua Through
2 Kings

We have already noted that the Deuteronomic idea is by no means confined to the book of Deuteronomy. Rather, it is widely understood as an ideology associated with a movement that, though originating at some time in the seventh century, continued into and perhaps beyond the exilic period. Its activity was highly influential, leaving its mark on many OT books. Therefore, a full account of it should arguably go beyond investigating Deuteronomy–2 Kings to look also at the prophets, and indeed Genesis–Numbers.

I intend, however, to pursue the Deuteronomic idea outside Deuteronomy only in Joshua–2 Kings, for several reasons. First, a treatment of these books has a natural primacy in our investigation because of the explicit links they form with Deuteronomy. These links exist not only at the level of ideas but also in scope and indeed in the story. Second, any hope of identifying Deuteronomic influence elsewhere in the OT depends on the definition given to it from a study of Deuteronomy–2 Kings. Admittedly, not all OT scholars admit to this thesis. The attempt some have made to distinguish between what is truly prophetic and what is Deuteronomic elaboration in a given prophetic book has proved difficult. It has led, in extreme cases, to calling material "Deuteronomic" that has no demonstrable substantial connection with the primary Deuteronomic corpus (Deuteronomy–2 Kings), even though other material in the same book is called Deuteronomic precisely because of such a connection. W. Thiel's influential treatment of Jeremiah is the prime example of this.[1] All such attempts fail in some measure, I believe, not only because of their illogicality, but also because they rarely show an appreciation of the sophistication of Deuteronomic thought, tending, quite wrongly, to equate it with banality of both style and substance.[2] Finally, I have elsewhere shown the individuality of the book of Jeremiah in relationship to Deuteronomic theology.[3]

THE ORIGIN OF JOSHUA–2 KINGS

The student of Joshua–2 Kings (DtH)[4] faces an acute problem in trying to establish the origin of the books. As we now have them, the books clearly tell a continuous, if uneven, story that spans the arrival of Israel under Joshua in the land

---

[1]W. Thiel, *Die deuteronomistische Redaktion von Jeremia 1–25* (Neukirchen: Neukirchener Verlag, 1973). R. R. Wilson's work on prophecy has highlighted the difficulty, it seems to me, of distinguishing between what he sees as the prophetic matrix of Deuteronomic thought in the so-called Ephraimite tradition of prophecy and Deuteronomic thought that is full grown; see, for example, his *Prophecy and Society in Ancient Israel* (Philadelphia: Fortress, 1980), pp. 225–52. Cf. also McKane's comment on Thiel, "Relations Between Poetry and Prose in the Book of Jeremiah with Special Reference to Jeremiah III 6-11 and XII 14-17," *SVT* 32 (1980), 224.

[2]See the account of this in L. Stulman, "The Prose Sermons of the Book of Jeremiah," SBLDS 83 (Atlanta: Scholars Press, 1986), 12–13, 16, 18.

[3]See my *Judgment and Promise: Interpreting the Book of Jeremiah* (Winona Lake, Ind.: Eisenbrauns/Leicester: Inter-Varsity, 1993).

[4]The treatment of this block of books normally excludes Ruth. This is partly because of the canonical tradition preserved in the Hebrew Bible that places this book in the Writings section, not in the Former Prophets. 1 Samuel, furthermore, forms a natural sequel to Judges. However, it must be admitted that the omission is in some measure simply a matter of scholarly convention.

of Canaan to the loss of the land in the twin exiles of northern "Israel" to Assyria and of southern "Judah" to Babylon. The story thus has a satisfying beginning and end (if only in the aesthetic sense!).

On the other hand, just because it extends over so long a period and purports to be an account of what actually happened at many different times, it was presumably composed of many different original fragments. Those fragments, furthermore, cannot easily be equated with the books into which the material has been divided since ancient times, for while Joshua and 1, 2 Samuel relate to relatively short periods, Judges and 1, 2 Kings clearly do not.

Two questions therefore arise: How may relatively early material be identified? and, What is the relationship between earlier and later material in the work as we have it today? Our interpretation of the books may well turn on our ability both to recognize the setting of the finished work and to understand what motivated its authors to use the material they inherited in the way in which they did.

The end of the story, the Babylonian exile of Judah, is the first unmistakable clue. More precisely, the last action in the drama is the release in 562 B.C. of King Jehoiachin, a prisoner in Babylon since his capture in 597 B.C. (2Ki 25:27–30). The perspective of 1, 2 Kings at least, then, seems to be the exilic period itself, more than two decades after the temple had fallen (586 B.C.) and while there was still no obvious prospect of the exile ending soon. Since the work of Noth, who believed DtH simply proclaimed the reasons for the catastrophe of exile in Israel's sin, it is this perspective that has been brought to bear on the question of why DtH was written.[5]

Analogies are immediately apparent with the problem of interpreting Deuteronomy. This book also spanned a period

---

[5]M. Noth, *The Deuteronomistic History* (Sheffield: JSOT, 1981); also see above, ch. 2.

of time from the verge of occupying the land to its final loss (at least in prospect, through its formal curses section; e.g., Dt 28:64–68). It too has raised in the minds of scholars the relationship between ancient traditions and a contemporary situation. And it too, as we saw, had led many interpreters to seek its *Sitz im Leben* in the period that culminated in the exile. DtH is different, however, for while Deuteronomy's setting remained elusive, Joshua–2 Kings offers a clear clue as to its *Sitz im Leben* by recounting events up to a point in the exilic period. Furthermore, by its character as a narrative of historical events, it presents us more palpably with the fact of early material somehow incorporated into a later work (or works).

That there is pre-exilic material in DtH is widely agreed. It will be worthwhile to highlight some points at which we may discern it. First, some parts appear to be ancient simply because they do not fit immediately into an exilic purpose to explain theologically the fall of Jerusalem. An example is the stories of Elijah and Elisha (1Ki 17–2Ki 9). These stories of healings and miraculous provision fit best into a period when prophecy was young in Israel and when the pressing issue was the survival of Yahwism in the face of strong competition from the religion of Baal. This is the natural background of the contest between Elijah and the prophets of Baal on Carmel (1Ki 18). The themes in these stories of fire, water, food, and life itself belong to a world in which a fundamental claim to control these things was being entered on behalf of Yahweh and against Baal.[6]

Older material can sometimes also be identified by the contrast it makes with stereotyped sections surrounding it, material that seems to betray the hand and purposes of the author or editor at that point. The book of Judges illustrates this. The story of Ehud, for example (Jdg 3:12–15), uses a

---

[6]L. Bronner, *The Stories of Elijah and Elisha* (Leiden: Brill, 1968), passim, especially 50–122.

style typical of the pattern in chs. 2–16 as a whole; the individuality and the color of 3:16–29, on the other hand, suggest that that part of the story had an independent existence from the interests of the editor of the whole book.[7] The poetic version of the Deborah story (Jdg 5) is often cited as one of the oldest pieces of writing in the OT.[8] Finally, some terms in Judges suggest a distance between the original narrative of an event and the later author or editor's telling of it. The phrase "to this day" (e.g., 1:21; 6:24; 18:12) is a case in point; an important variation of this is the phrase "until the time of the captivity of the land" (18:30), suggesting a date close to the last days of the northern kingdom.[9]

A second feature that points to an early period in Israel's history is the controversy over the monarchy. When the people demand that Samuel give them a king, there is a hostile response both from Samuel himself and from Yahweh, who regards it as a rejection of him as their King (1Sa 8:4–9; see also Dt 33:5; Jdg 8:23; 9:7–15). It was long customary to interpret 1Sa 8–12 as containing a debate within early Israel about the rightness of kingship, and the chapters were divided into alleged pro- and anti-monarchical sources.[10] Today this source division seems less likely because of more careful studies of the narrative.[11] Nevertheless, it remains

---

[7]On the editing of Judges see Noth, *The Deuteronomistic History*; J. A. Soggin, *Judges*, OTL (London: SCM, 1981), 5–6; A. D. H. Mayes, *The Story of Israel from Settlement to Exile* (London: SCM, 1983), 58–80. Lengthy treatments may be found in W. Richter, *Traditionsgeschichtliche Untersuchungen zum Richterbuch* (Bonn: P. Hanstein, 1963) and *Die Bearbeitung des "Retterbuches" in der deuteronomistischen Epoche* (Bonn: P. Hanstein, 1964).

[8]Soggin, *Judges*, 92.

[9]Soggin uses 18:27–31 as a "kind of *hieros logos* of the overthrow—the reason for Dan's destruction in 734–732"; ibid., 278.

[10]M. Buber was an early exponent of this view; see *The Kingship of God* (London: Allen and Unwin, 1967), 83; cf. O. Eissfeldt, *Die Composition der Samuelisbücher* (Leipzig: Hinrichs, 1931), 6–11. Buber's analysis is interesting in itself, however, for his understanding of Judges and Samuel as the biblical "politeia" (p. 84).

[11]E. M. Good, *Irony in the Old Testament* (London: SPCK, 1965), 56–80; R. P. Gordon, *1 and 2 Samuel* (Exeter: Paternoster, 1986), 26–35; V. P. Long,

probable that the recorded hostility to the institution of kingship represents actual resistance to its acceptance into an Israel that had a strong tribal, non-monarchical tradition.[12] One of the remarkable features of 1, 2 Samuel, indeed, is the paradox of their initial reluctance to countenance kingship together with their enthusiastic reception of it in 2 Samuel 7, the dynastic promise to David. This high point, furthermore, gives way again to ambivalence because of David's adulterous relationship with Bathsheba and its baneful consequences in civil war with Absalom (2Sa 11–20). The roller-coaster changes in the face of kingship presented in Samuel are likely to reflect the rough course of its actual reception into Israel.

The third indication that there is ancient material in DtH relates to the story just referred to, David's relationship with Bathsheba, and the section often known as the Succession Narrative (SN; 2Sa 9–20; 1Ki 1–2). Early in the present century, L. Rost identified these chapters as a self-contained narrative that had all the marks of an authentic account of contemporary events.[13] He based his argument on the apparent historical interest and character of the writing and its apparent intimate knowledge of the time and court of David. Rost's analysis no longer enjoys the popularity it once did, for a number of reasons. Literary studies have shown that SN does not make a clean new beginning at 9:1, but is connected with preceding material; furthermore, chs. 21–24,

---

The Reign and Rejection of King Saul (Atlanta: Scholars Press, 1989), 173–233. Cf. L. Eslinger, *The Kingship of God in Crisis* (Sheffield: JSOT, 1985), 44–62.

[12]See the recent treatment of anti-monarchical texts by F. Crüsemann, *Der Widerstand gegen das Königtum* (Neukirchen: Neukirchener Verlag, 1978). He basically follows Eissfeldt on the literary criticism of 1Sa 8–12, locating anti-monarchical feeling in a resistance to the early monarchy that strove to restore pre-state conditions (pp. 122–27). As a result, kingly rule in Israel was always limited (pp. 125–26). For Israel as essentially non-monarchical, see C. J. H. Wright, *God's People in God's Land: Family, Land and Property in the Old Testament* (Grand Rapids: Eerdmans, 1990), who drew in measure on N. K. Gottwald's *The Tribes of Yahweh* (Maryknoll, NY: Orbis, 1979).

[13]L. Rost, *The Succession to the Throne of David* (Sheffield: Almond, 1982; first German edition, Stuttgart: Kohlhammer, 1926), 104–5.

omitted from SN by Rost as different in character and purpose, is being reinstated as an integral part of the Samuel narrative.[14] On other grounds, SN is presently being dated at different times and is thought to have been motivated by political objectives, related in one way or another to the memory of David but not necessarily contemporary with him.[15] Again, J. Van Seters has dated SN in the late monarchy in the context of a sophisticated argument that history writing arises in Israel only with Dtr.[16]

The antiquity of SN cannot be decided, it is true, on the grounds of its history-likeness alone. Those who look to other periods than that of David himself, however, have to propose some convincing alternative setting. This in turns depends on an interpretation of the material. Van Seters, for example, rests much of his argument on his belief that Dtr idealizes David and would not have incorporated SN into his work. Its inclusion must therefore have come later. This, however, begs an important question about the purpose of DtH as a whole, a question that has, I believe, more subtlety in its appraisal of David than van Seters has allowed.

A final indication of ancient material in DtH relates to Jerusalem as the chosen place of worship. It is clear that in 1, 2 Kings Jerusalem is regarded as having absolute priority in matters of worship. It is expressly identified in 2 Kings 21:7 as Yahweh's "chosen" place (using the terms of Dt 12:5, etc.), and at 1 Kings 3:2 the author feels constrained to explain the prevalent worship at high places by pointing out that the temple at Jerusalem had not yet been built. Working backwards chronologically, Jerusalem obviously leaps to

---

[14]R. A. Carlson, *David: The Chosen King* (Stockholm: Almqvist and Wikseel, 1964), 26; Brueggemann, "2 Samuel 21–24: An Appendix of Deconstruction?" *CBQ* 50 (1988), 383–97.

[15]D. M. Gunn, *The Story of King David* (Sheffield: JSOT, 1978), 30–34; W. H. Whybray, *The Succession Narrative* (London: SCM, 1986), 54–55.

[16]J. van Seters, *In Search of History* (New Haven: Yale Univ. Press, 1983), 277–90.

importance in 2 Samuel, when David makes that city his capital and locates the ark there (2Sa 5–6). Before 2 Samuel, however, Jerusalem has little significance in the narrative. Throughout Joshua and Judges it remains Canaanite Jebus, one of the cities of the hill country that Israel was unable to take following its entry to the land (Jos 15:63; Jdg 1:21).

The obscurity of Jerusalem in Joshua and Judges might in theory be explained simply in terms of the logic of the narrative itself: The people's promised "rest" from their enemies (Dt 12:9) came about only when David was in possession of Jerusalem (2Sa 7:1; cf. Ps 132:14). It does seem to be true that DtH as a whole understands the development of Israel's history of worship in this way (no less is implied by 2Sa 7:1 and 1Ki 3:2). However, this is not the whole story, for a memory persists in the material that Israel had in fact worshiped at other places before Jerusalem came to press its claim. The importance of Shechem at the time of entry to the land (Jos 8:30–35; cf. Dt 27), the later prominence of Shiloh (Jos 18:8–10; 1Sa 1–3; note the "temple" in 1:9; cf. Jer 7:12–15), the note that the ark stood at one time at Bethel (Jdg 20:27), and the reaffirmation of the kingship at Gilgal in the time of Saul (1Sa 11:14–15) are among the data that led a generation of scholars to believe that in early Israel a number of sanctuaries enjoyed pre-eminence at different periods.[17]

The story in Joshua 22 is perhaps as significant as any of this material, for the issue there is precisely the importance of a central place of worship for all the tribes, marked out by its possession of the ark, but where the sanctuary in question is Shiloh (vv. 10–12). While Noth's general theory of an "amphictyony" rightly met severe criticism in due course, there remains good evidence of a tendency towards some kind

---

[17]See above, ch. 2, n. 37, for references to A. Alt and G. von Rad; see also F. Dumermuth, "Zur deuteronomischen Kulttheologie und ihren Voraussetzungen," ZAW 70 (1958), 59–98. The most influential argument for this view came from M. Noth, Das System der zwölf Stämme Israels (Stuttgart: Kohlhammer, 1930).

of unified worship in early Israel. It is unlikely that this picture would have been invented by an author who was anxious to promote the sole legitimacy of the Jerusalem temple. DtH therefore presents data analogous to the appearance of Shechem in Deuteronomy 27, in the sense that the latter highlights the difficulty of thinking that Deuteronomy was written from the perspective of a party promoting Jerusalem. Though ultimately emanating from Jerusalem (now understood as Yahweh's "chosen place"), DtH contains evidence of a long history of earlier traditions.

THE DEUTERONOMIC HISTORY: THE PARTS AND THE WHOLE

Our next question is whether DtH as a whole may be said to have a unified purpose or meaning. If so, then it can only be discovered by establishing how the various parts that go to make it up have been brought into the present work, and by analyzing whether this process was done according to an identifiable theological program. Does DtH, in fact, have a unity, or is it merely a collection of disparate elements? The question is an inevitable part of our search for the meaning of "Deuteronomic" theology; on it depends whether there is such a thing at all, or whether we are dealing with a cluster of loosely related "theologies."

There are, in fact, certain indications that DtH has a unity of some sort. The most obvious indications concern two facets of its relationship with Deuteronomy: the manner in which the story continues and the typical ideas that are contained in both. The continuing storyline is clearest at the "joints" between the books. Deuteronomy prepares for the post-Mosaic era by introducing Joshua as the new leader (Dt 31:1–8; 34), a succession that the book of Joshua in turn recalls (Jos 1:1–9). At the same time Joshua acknowledges the "Book of the Law" (v. 8), presumably meaning Deuteronomy. In addition, the command given to Israel in Deuter-

onomy 27 concerning ceremonies to be performed on Mount
Ebal and Mount Gerizim (at Shechem) is reported to have
been carried out in Joshua 8:30–35, with an express allusion
to the command in Deuteronomy 27 (see Jos 8:33b). The
book of Joshua as a whole, furthermore, tells the story of the
possession of the land that Deuteronomy had set before Israel
as both promise and project.

In a similar way, Judges opens with an allusion to the
death of Joshua and continues with its own development of
the story of the conquest.[18] In turn, the refrain in its closing
chapters, "In those days Israel had no king; everyone did as
he saw fit" (21:25; cf. 18:1; 19:1), prepares for the story of the
origin of kingship in Israel, precisely the subject of 1 Samuel.
A close connection is forged between 1, 2 Samuel by David's
lament for Saul and Jonathan (2Sa 1:7–27), and the theme of
kingship is then taken forward with the dynastic promise to
David (2Sa 7:8–17) and its aftermath. The book of 1 Kings
sees Solomon safely on the throne, a culmination of the story
of David and his sons in 2 Samuel 11–20, and 1 Kings 1–2
explicitly lays to rest certain elements in that story—and
indeed some of its characters! (1Ki 1:5–9, 19–25, 36–46).

The connections between the individual books of DtH
(and Deuteronomy) can be illustrated in other, slightly
different, ways. One unifying thread is formed by a series of
promises and their fulfillments. The most obvious example is,
of course, Deuteronomy's promise of land, fulfilled in Joshua.
Another is the promise of "rest from enemies," associated

---

[18]It has often been said that Joshua and Judges contain conflicting
accounts of the conquest of the land. They can be viewed, however, as
complementary, Joshua stressing the fulfillment of the Deuteronomic
promise, while Judges focuses on Israel's failure to take the land completely
because of incomplete faith and obedience. In fact there is considerable
agreement between the two books when the details are examined closely.
Joshua is like Judges in showing at crucial points that the land was not
completely subdued by Joshua (13:1–7, 13; 15:63; 16:10; 17:12–13). See
also R. Polzin's treatment of Joshua and Judges as manifesting a unity of
concept (*Moses and the Deuteronomist* [New York: Seabury, 1980], 73–204).

with the finding of the place that Yahweh would choose for his worship (Dt 12:5-11). This promise is regarded as fulfilled when David at last completely subdues the land (2Sa 7:1), where, of course, it is associated with the establishment of Jerusalem (now finally wrested from the Jebusites; see 2Sa 5:6-10; cf. Jos 15:63; Jdg 1:21) as the proper place of worship of Yahweh by reason of the presence of the ark there (2Sa 6). Again, the time of prosperity and peace granted to Solomon that allowed him to build the temple (2Ki 5-8) fulfills the promise to David at the time when he himself was prohibited from doing so (note the allusion to 2Sa 7:13 in 1Ki 5:3-5). These examples are important because they span the different books, showing that in some sense there is conscious development from one to another. The same phenomenon also occurs within books, especially in 1, 2 Kings (the division between which is rather artificial), for example in the prediction, generations before the event, of Josiah's destruction of Jeroboam's sanctuary at Bethel (1Ki 13:2; cf. 2Ki 23:15-16).

Other connections between books are not necessarily in terms of promise and fulfillment. For example, there is a reminiscence in 2 Samuel 21:1-6 of Joshua's covenant with the Canaanite population of Gibeon (Jos 9), itself an offence against the command of Deuteronomy 7:2.

Connections echoing across the narrative other than those just illustrated occur in terms of theological structuring. Scholars have drawn attention to the significance of speeches in this respect, specifically to covenantal addresses by the leaders of Israel at important junctures of the narrative. Examples are Joshua's farewell speech of exhortation to the tribes (Jos 23), followed by his covenant-renewal at Shechem (Jos 24); Samuel's address following his acceptance in principle of kingship in Israel (1Sa 12); and Solomon's prayer at the dedication of the newly-built temple (1Ki 8:15-53).[19]

[19]The point was made by M. Noth, *The Deuteronomistic History*, 5-6.

These imply the unity of the narrative, not merely in a formal way, but also in their expression of its character, by means of their covenantal language, as Deuteronomic.

The above signs of the unity of the whole work are, in one way or another, features of the narrative. The second kind of unity in DtH is in terms of theology. This indeed is what is chiefly implied by the idea of a "Deuteronomic History." Inevitably, it has been adumbrated by our discussion of narrative features. The theological ideas in question are essentially those that we have seen in Deuteronomy. Chief among these is Israel's possession of the land and the conditions on which this can be realized and maintained. In Judges, for example, the land is held intermittently and in varying degrees according to the faithfulness of Israel to Yahweh.[20] In 2 Kings, of course, it is finally lost. The typical failure of Israel highlighted in 1, 2 Kings is their idolatry, the sin par excellence according to Deuteronomy (Dt 7:1–5; 13; cf. 1Ki 11:1–10).

Leadership in Israel is another theological topic that links Deuteronomy and the succeeding books. Deuteronomy's institution of elders and judges (Dt 1:9–18; 17:8–13), along with its general egalitarian understanding of Israel,[21] is a function of its understanding of God as Israel's king (33:5). Deuteronomy, therefore, cannot brook any royal tyranny such as typified the nations surrounding Israel; it countenances a king at all only in a restricted sense, subordinating him to the law and stressing his "brotherhood" in Israel (17:14–20).[22] This orientation of Deuteronomy forms the background to the hot issue in Judges about the nature of leadership—explaining, for example, Gideon's refusal to

---

[20]B. Webb in *The Book of the Judges* (Sheffield: JSOT, 1987) demonstrates this observation with great cogency.

[21]See McConville, *Law and Theology in Deuteronomy* (Sheffield, JSOT, 1984), 19–20, for the importance of the idea of "brotherhood" in Deuteronomy.

[22]See the discussion of this idea in ch. 2, above.

accept the title of king (Jdg 8:22–23) and Samuel's anger at the people's demand for one in 1 Samuel 8. The picture of tyranny in 1 Samuel 8:11–18 is precisely what Deuteronomy 17:14–20 aimed to prevent, and of course is a tragically accurate prediction of what the monarchy at its worst, both north and south, would bring. At these points, DtH is of one mind with Deuteronomy. (The question whether DtH is entirely united in its view of kingship is complicated and will be returned to below).

More generally, the theological links between Deuteronomy and DtH can be expressed as covenantal. The story of covenant undergoes a development from Deuteronomy, when it incorporates the idea of kingship into the scheme of things, to 1 Samuel 11:14, where the renewal of the kingdom is a covenant-renewal that gives Saul, as king, a place within the covenant arrangements.[23] The nature of covenant in DtH is complicated by the look of unconditionality about the promise to David in 2 Samuel 7:8–17. However, the impression is rectified by the explicit language of 1 Kings 2:2–4, which ensures that the covenant with David must be understood along good Deuteronomic lines.

As we continue to build up a picture of "Deuteronomic Theology," our next task will be to examine some of the ways in which scholars have attempted to account for the unities in Deuteronomy and DtH. In doing so, however, we must not pre-judge whether the different books that compose DtH might have distinctive theological concerns of their own, distinguishing them from each other. In fact, it is likely that there is a certain tension between the individuality of the books and their belonging in the larger work. This tension was felt by von Rad, for example, who thought of Judges and Kings as "Deuteronomistic," yet drew attention to differences between them that he thought precluded the conclusion that

---

[23]See W. J. Dumbrell, *Covenant and Creation* (Exeter: Paternoster, 1984), 135–36, on this passage.

they had been produced as a single work.[24] His view has gained support more recently from B. Webb.[25] The present writer has argued elsewhere that 1, 2 Kings deliberately refrain from expressing the full hope for a future beyond exile that is found in Deuteronomy 30:1–10.[26] The point must await further development below, however.

THE DEUTERONOMIC HISTORY IN MODERN SCHOLARSHIP

In recent times, scholarship has largely attempted to explain DtH as a continuous whole, while at the same time accounting for diversity within it. Noth's idea of a single Deuteronomist working in the exilic period, discussed above,[27] stressed strongly the work's unity of conception as an explanation of the judgment of exile. Successors, however, thought that this did not account for the notes of future hope that are struck at certain points, especially in the dynastic promise to David (2Sa 7). Von Rad dissented from Noth on this point, believing that this promise represented one aspect of the theology of the work that could not simply be set aside.[28] Noth's idea that Dtr had felt obliged to preserve material that he had inherited, even though he did not agree with it, is unconvincing.[29] However, the recognition of different thrusts within the books was not the solution of a problem, but merely its definition. It posed the question how

---

[24]G. von Rad, *Old Testament Theology* (London: Oliver and Boyd, 1962), 1:346–47.

[25]B. Webb, *Judges*, 211.

[26]See my "1 Kings VIII 46-53 and the Deuteronomic Hope," *VT* 42 (1992), 67–79.

[27]See the discussion in ch. 2.

[28]See G. von Rad, *Studies in Deuteronomy* (London: SCM, 1953), 74–91.

[29]F. M. Cross, *Canaanite Myth and Hebrew Epic* (Cambridge, Mass.: Harvard Univ. Press, 1973), 275–76. Von Rad's idea of a two-sided message of promise and judgment is better-conceived (*Studies in Deuteronomy*, 89).

such emphases could be found together within a work that has, as we have just seen, undeniable marks of unity.

F. M. Cross and I. W. Provan

Explanations after Noth have mostly fallen into two main types, each in its own way indebted to Noth. The first is associated with F. M. Cross, who proposed two editions of the work, the first from the time of Josiah and optimistic in tone, the second exilic. The latter was a recasting of the existing work in the light of the disappointments of the years following Josiah's promising resistance of imperial power. Obviously, Cross's "Dtr2" closely resembles Noth's single Dtr.

Cross's separation of the two editions is based on literary criticism as well as historical criticism. Second Kings 23:25–27 is a crucial text for him, for he sees in it an impossible contradiction in the context of a unified work. In one breath King Josiah is hailed as the greatest of all Davidic kings (v. 25), and in the next a final sentence is passed on the kingdom of Judah because of the sins of Manasseh, Josiah's predecessor but one (vv. 26–27).[30] The force of Cross's point should not be underestimated. Josiah's reform comes as the culmination of a major strand in 1, 2 Kings. First, it seems to offer a satisfying resolution of the dynastic promise to David, explicitly invoked in Dtr's exaltation of Josiah. The point is strengthened by the manner in which Solomon is stripped of ten tribes and left one (in addition to Judah) "for the sake of Jerusalem, which I have chosen" (1Ki 11:13), a qualification of the condemnation of Solomon that appears to leave a door open for the later fulfillment of the Davidic promise in Judah. Second, the reform is prophesied in 1 Kings 13:2–3, so that this passage together with the account of the reform (2Ki 22–23) becomes a promise-fulfillment arc that spans the whole monarchy period after Solomon and most of the 1, 2 Kings.

---

[30]Cross, *Canaanite Myth*, 285–86.

Third, the story of Josiah's reform itself is told with such fanfare, more so than previous reforms (e.g., that of Hezekiah, 2Ki 18:4), that it draws attention to itself as the apex in the narrative of the promise to David. All this makes the idea of a purely pessimistic narrative look fragile. Cross therefore drew his conclusion about two editions, as outlined above.

Although Cross has had enthusiastic followers,[31] the theory is seriously handicapped, primarily because its dependence on 2 Kings 23:25–27 is not informed by any systematic study of that text in its context in 1, 2 Kings. In fact, a careful reading of the two books of Kings from the moment of Solomon's accession shows that the narrative has an ironical aspect, one that leads the reader to fear that the best hopes for Judah might in the end be frustrated.[32] The jarring climax of the account of Josiah's noble deeds belongs to the style and structure that the author has adopted for his purpose.[33]

A recent variation of Cross's theory deserves consideration at this point. I. W. Provan has made a new argument for a double edition of DtH, holding that the first leads up to the account of Hezekiah in 2 Kings 18–19, though written in the time of Josiah. In this edition, a crucial distinction is maintained between the northern and southern kingdoms on the basis of the unconditional promise to David. Hezekiah is thus seen as the king in whom the dynastic promise is conspicuously fulfilled. This edition knows 1, 2 Samuel substantially in their present form, though without their antimonarchical sections. The second edition, in contrast, makes

---

[31]They include A. D. H. Mayes, *The Story of Israel from Settlement to Exile*, 13–14; N. Lohfink, "Zur neueren Diskussion über 2 Kön 22-23," in *Das Deuteronomium: Entstehung, Gestalt und Botschaft*, ed. N. Lohfink (Leuven: Leuven Univ. Press, 1965), 45.

[32]I have developed this point in "Narrative and Meaning in the Books of Kings," *Biblica* 70 (1989), 31–49.

[33]The best account of the matter is that of H.-D. Hoffmann, *Reform und Reformen: Untersuchungen zu einem Grundthema der deuteronomistischen Geschichtsschreibung* (Zurich, Theologischer Verlag, 1980).

disobedience to the Mosaic law the decisive factor in Judah's history.

The argument rests to a large extent on studies of texts concerning the "high places" and texts about David himself. Regarding the high places, Provan sees a difference between texts before Hezekiah, which he believes are concerned only with the need for centralization, and later texts, in which a hostility to idolatry comes to the fore. His analysis of the passages that qualify the faithfulness of certain "good" kings, such as Asa, with a phrase "although" or "however" (Heb. *raq*; 1Ki 15:14; cf. 3:2; 22:43), is used to support his view that in the pre-Hezekiah narrative the failure to remove the high places is only moderately serious and that the motif is a function of the aspiration to centralization of the cult.[34] The Josiah narrative cannot be the climax of this seam, because there the high places are evidently regarded as idolatrous.[35] As for the David texts, Hezekiah is seen as the natural culmination of the affirmations that God would always keep a "lamp" for himself in Jerusalem, a theme that appears for the last time at 2 Kings 8:19. Furthermore, the realization of the Davidic ideal is said to be at home in connection with Hezekiah (2Ki 18:3), but only secondary in connection with Josiah (2Ki 22:2).[36]

A full response to Provan is beyond our scope here. Nevertheless, in general I believe his thesis is open to the same criticisms as that of Cross. The central question is one of method in approaching the narrative. Provan has applied source- and form-critical analysis in a way that has diverted attention from important features of 1, 2 Kings as narrative. His treatment of individual texts is capable of quite different interpretations. For example, the passages with *raq*, qualify-

---

[34]I. W. Provan, *Hezekiah and the Books of Kings* (Berlin: de Gruyter, 1988), 62–69.

[35]Ibid., 82–84.

[36]Ibid.

ing the congratulation of kings, can be seen (as I think they should) not as an excuse, but as an ominous sign.[37]

A proper interpretation of these and other details of the narrative must rest on recognizing certain features that are discernible only on the broad canvas. This is to advocate a significantly different approach from Provan's (as from Cross's). Provan's interpretation is unconvincing on two crucial points. First, far from setting a double standard for north and south respectively, 1, 2 Kings shows, I believe, a progressive blurring of the difference between them. The south's infatuation with the ways of Ahab becomes a determining factor in its fate. Second, the wedge that Provan forces between the portrayals of Hezekiah and Josiah is unconvincing. He fails to see the deliberate ambiguities in the portrayal of the former and to acknowledge how these ambiguities find echoes in the account of the latter. Hezekiah is in reality a preparation for Josiah. The promise of a permanent Davidic Reich will prove to be an illusion, and it is impossible to isolate a strand of 1, 2 Kings that does not know this.[38]

These comments on the nature of the narrative of 1, 2 Kings apply to Cross as much as to Provan. The solution, of which their respective works are variations, has a further feature that makes it vulnerable to criticism, namely, its theological polarization. Their approach, indeed, is reminiscent of approaches that we noted at an earlier stage in relation to Deuteronomy. Here once again we find the messages of grace and promise on the one hand, and law and judgment on the other forced apart—gratuitously in my view. Here as there, I believe the relationship between law and grace is more subtle.

---

[37]See my argument in "Narrative and Meaning in Kings," especially 35–38.

[38]Ibid. The point is developed at great length by Hoffmann, *Reform und Reformen*, especially 146ff. Hoffmann thinks DtH presents Hezekiah, Manasseh, and Josiah as a "Trias" of great reformers.

R. Smend

We turn now to a second approach to the problem of reconciling the themes of promise and judgment in DtH (though it has important aspects in common with the first, and our evaluation of Cross somewhat anticipates what follows). The view in question is associated with R. Smend. Where Cross thought in terms of a first edition of DtH lightly overlaid with a second, Smend proposed a more thorough-going and subtle interweaving of redactional layers. His first (DtrG) is the basic history, optimistic and confident in tone; it assumes that the conquest of the land is complete. His second layer (DtrN) is a legalistic (nomistic) expansion. In this one, the conquest is incomplete and the tenure of the land insecure; it has a strong flavor of conditionality and an emphasis on the law.[39] Disciples of Smend, notably W. Dietrich, have proposed an intermediate, "prophetic" layer (DtrP), and this idea of a threefold redaction became the form in which the theory has been perpetuated.[40]

Here too, however, the literary-critical criteria suffer from close inspection, and the explanation of the theological poles of the discourse as rival points of view enshrined in successive redactions precludes the recognition of theological profundity. Smend's analysis of five passages in Joshua and Judges rested excessively on two-edged stylistic criteria.[41] The

---

[39]R. Smend, "Das Gesetz und die Völker," in H. W. Wolff, ed., *Probleme Biblischer Theologie* (Munich: Kaiser, 1971), 494–509.

[40]W. Dietrich, *Prophetie und Geschichte* (Göttingen: Vandenhoeck and Ruprecht, 1972); cf. T. Veijola, *Die Ewige Dynastie* (Helsinki: Suomalainen Tiedeakatemia, 1975), and *Das Königtum in der Beurteilung der deuteronomistischen Historiographie* (Helsinki: Suomalainen Tiedeakatemia, 1977).

[41]T. Veijola declares in one place that style is the only criterion for determining the history of redaction (*Das Königtum*, 13). In another place, however, he is compelled to admit that "one cannot expect [the presence of peculiar characteristics of DtrN] in every text, as the deuteronomists, of course, did not only speak with their own phraseology," ibid., 110–11. This is precisely the "heads I win, tails you lose" thinking that McKane criticized in Thiel's work on Jeremiah; see note 1.

consequence is the casting of a mold into which any pericope can then be poured. Lohfink, criticizing H. Spieckermann's treatment of 2 Kings 23, concludes: "The truth is that he knew too well in advance that the entities 'DtrH' [= DtrG], 'DtrP' and 'DtrN' existed, and how one is obliged to go about distributing the material to them."[42]

A fundamental difficulty attaches, furthermore, to the view entailed by Smend's theory that all three redactional layers belong to the exilic period. The exilic situation is thus made the scene of a remarkable amount of rival literary productivity, without any historical evidence for the existence of the kinds of parties that the theory postulates, or any serious explanation of how the successive redactions might have become accepted by the exilic community.

For these reasons, it should not be surprising to find that the theory produces improbabilities at the level of detailed interpretation. A tendency to produce false distinctions is illustrated by T. Veijola's understanding of the Davidic dynasty. For him, DtrG always portrays David as innocent and pious. DtrP, in contrast, is quite negative about the dynasty (e.g., 2Sa 12:1–14). Finally, DtrN reverts to a pro-dynastic stance, albeit with nomistic strings attached.[43] It takes unusual confidence for a historian to perform such disentanglements. Veijola even claims to discern that DtrN adopted his pro-Davidic stance against his better judgment, compelled as he was to depict David relatively favorably because of his opposition to Saul, but covering himself by depicting David as an exception, by whose measure others might be found wanting.[44] All this is quite fanciful.

Smend's theory suffers in the end from two fatal weaknesses. First, like that of Cross, it has an inadequate understanding of the subtle ironies of the literature; ideas that

---

[42]Lohfink, "Zur neueren Diskussion über 2 Kön 22-23," 44.

[43]Veijola, *Die Ewige Dynastie*, 130, 139–40, 142. Cf. Dietrich, *Prophetie und Geschichte*, 142–43; Mayes, *The Story of Israel from Settlement to Exile*, 136–37.

[44]Veijola, *Die Ewige Dynastie*, 118–19.

seem to be in tension with each other are parcelled out to different propagandists. Second, there is no plausible explanation for the portrayal of Josiah. Its likeliest originator, according to the hypothesis, is DtrG. Yet it strains the imagination to believe that a picture of Josiah that was wholly unqualified in its enthusiasm, as the theory demands, might have been promoted or accepted by anyone in the exile. In reality, any exilic portrayal of Josiah that did not try to account for the events that followed his death would be nonsensical.

We have now seen two major attempts in the wake of Noth to account for the tension between promise/grace and law/judgment in DtH. Both have been found wanting, partly because of a too ready polarization of ideas, which has in turn preempted a more penetrating theological enquiry. A satisfying explanation of Deuteronomic theology in Joshua–2 Kings has to provide a better account of the ending of 2 Kings and, as I have suggested above, requires reading the books on a broad canvas and in their own terms. This implies a return to the view that 1, 2 Kings has a unified message.

H.-D. Hoffmann and T. R. Hobbs

If Noth failed to convince in his theory of a single Deuteronomist, others, notably H.-D. Hoffmann and T. R. Hobbs, have made progress in this respect. It is important to notice how their approaches to the literature differ from those of Cross and others. Both these scholars find the Babylonian exile anticipated throughout 1, 2 Kings. For Hoffmann, the story of Solomon already bodes ill, his notorious second period (2Ki 11) being anticipated already in the conditionality of 2:1–4; 3:4–15; and 9:4–9. All subsequent kings, he argues, show signs of kinship with Solomon in his second period, until Josiah, when it is too late.[45] Hoffmann contends

---

[45]Hoffmann, *Reform und Reformen*, 50–56; cf. T. R. Hobbs, in *2 Kings*, WBC (Waco, Texas: Word, 1985): "The ultimate destruction of Jerusalem is only a matter of time" (p. xxv).

that the storyline of 1, 2 Kings focuses on reforms, not just of "good" kings, but also of the villains. Thus while Asa is a Yahweh-reformer, Ahab is a "reformer" too, in his promotion of the cult of Baal! While Asa stands at the beginning of a line that leads to Hezekiah (and Josiah),[46] Ahab leads to Manasseh.[47] The progressive influence of the north, especially Ahab, upon the south is a crucial part of the ruin of the latter.[48] 2 Kings 17 is unified and integral (apart from vv. 34–41, but including the crucial vv. 19–20), and thus the condemnation of the north serves properly, and not merely secondarily, as an adumbration of the fate of the south.[49] The story of the book thus consists in a counterpoint that comes to a dramatic climax in the alternation of the most extreme forms of each contrary tendency (Ahaz-Hezekiah-Manasseh-Josiah).[50]

In the final stage of his argument, Hoffmann demonstrates that the story of reform from Hezekiah through Manasseh to Josiah has a unity and brings the whole narrative to its climax. Here, the dual possibilities of positive and negative cult-reform are focused with intensity. The increasing momentum of the "pendulum-swings" from one extreme to the other signals that the finale is near. The Manasseh account forms links both backwards in the story with the allusion to Ahab (2Ki 21:3), and forwards to Josiah. A corollary is that the author's explanation of the coming exile in terms of Manasseh's sins (2Ki 23:25–27; see ch. 21) is not a secondary addition to DtrG, but integral to the narrative. To prove the point he shows a whole web of cross-references that he sees as the special literary achievement of

---

[46]To be precise, Hoffmann omits Josiah from the pattern as he describes it, thinking that his story has a special place in the structure of the books. This is probably an unnecessary refinement of the argument, however.

[47]Hoffmann, *Reform und Reformen*, 78–82.

[48]Ibid., 97.

[49]Ibid., 127–30. Cf. again Hobbs (*2 Kings*, 241), who sees the chapter as a view of the fall of the north from the perspective of the (now fallen) south.

[50]Hoffmann, *Reform und Reformen*, 146–55.

the single author (DtrG).[51] The force of this analysis shows that the Manasseh explanation is no mere afterthought crudely grafted on to a triumphalist document. Rather, the "success" of Josiah is part of a story that is ultimately one of failure.

The role of Hezekiah as a prototype of Josiah is equally important. Where Cross thought DtrG played Hezekiah down, the more to enhance Josiah's glory, Hoffmann and Hobbs accentuate the parallels between the two. Like his more celebrated descendant, Hezekiah too carried out a reform that draws no qualification from DtrG in his recounting of it (Hezekiah *did* remove the high places), yet one that gives way not to peace and prosperity, but to nothing but trouble.[52] Hobbs adds important observations about the relation of the reprieve of Hezekiah from death (2Ki 20:6) and the delayed judgment on Judah.[53] In each case the reprieve is merely temporary. The ominous visit of the Babylonian emissaries (2Ki 20) fits well into the purpose of the author when it is understood in this manner.[54] Once again, then, there is a pointer in the body of DtH to the final outcome for Judah.

When the account of Josiah has been thus prepared for, its ambiguities, which Cross had thought impossible, can be seen to be part of its essential nature. As Hezekiah's reform had produced no ultimate good for Judah, so is it with Josiah's. Huldah's oracle (2Ki 22:15–20) proclaims the fall of Judah before Josiah's measures begin, and the premature death of the king is in keeping with it.[55]

---

[51]Ibid., 161–63; note especially the table of cross-references on p. 163.

[52]For Hoffmann's ideas on the close parallels between Hezekiah and Josiah, see n. 38, above.

[53]Hobbs, *2 Kings*, xxxvi, 287–88.

[54]The passage was a distinct embarrassment to the theory of F. M. Cross, as is evident from the attempt of R. D. Nelson to explain it (*The Double Redaction of the Deuteronomistic History* [Sheffield: JSOT, 1981], 129–32). See my comments in "Narrative and Meaning in Kings," 43.

[55]Scholarship has generally regarded Huldah's oracle as inaccurate on the matter of Josiah's death (and therefore likely to be authentic!), because

The argument for the unity of the story of cult-reforms in 1, 2 Kings is completed by a demonstration of the continuity between Josiah's reform and all previous reforms. That account, indeed, can be seen as a totaling of all individual cult-notices previously used in 1, 2 Kings: "Aus den Reformen die Reform."[56]

As an understanding of the narrative of 1, 2 Kings, Hoffmann's work is more persuasive than those that try to explain its tensions by resorting to source or redaction criticism. Despite this demonstration, however, his understanding of the message of the book is a curious anticlimax. He contends that Josiah, the righteous king par excellence, arrives on the scene of Judah's history too late to make a difference.[57] Dtr intends, he thinks, to make Josiah a model of obedience to the law, for the benefit of the exilic community.[58] This understanding of Josiah, however, leaves the question of why Hezekiah's reforming zeal was not adequate to turn the history of Judah. More importantly, it is difficult to see in what sense a member of a now-defunct dynasty can function as a model for a kingless exilic community. Finally, the idea fails to take seriously the problem posed in 1, 2 Kings about the failure of the monarchy itself in the light of the dynastic promise to David.

Hoffmann is unsatisfactory on the interpretation of DtH because he has, in the end, accepted uncritically the premise

---

the promise that he would be buried "in peace" (*shalom*) seems to fit ill with his tragic fall in battle (2Ki 23:29). See J. Gray, *I and II Kings*, 3d ed., OTL (London: SCM, 1977), 661. Hoffmann is right, I think, in his argument that the oracle assures Josiah only that he will not see the coming devastation of his country, *Reform und Reformen*, 183–87. Proper burial is an important consideration in 1, 2 Kings (several indeed were not buried: Jeroboam, Baasha, Ahab); Huldah's promise to Josiah is therefore not trivial.

[56]"Out of the reforms, the Reform;" Hoffmann, *Reform und Reformen*, 251–61.

[57]Ibid., 56.

[58]Ibid., 270.

that DtH is the product of the Josianic reform program, a view that I think his own work actually undermines. From the fact that reforms in 1, 2 Kings typically fail to secure the covenantal blessings for Judah it follows, not that a better reform might have done the trick (which patently it did not), but that none ever could. The brilliant portrayal of Josiah's efforts makes this point with irony and force.

With this conclusion we are close to an interpretation of 1, 2 Kings in general, and thus to an understanding of what might constitute the "Deuteronomic" idea in their case. These books may be said to promote the ideals of Deuteronomy, first, in their concern for right worship, reflected in the belief that Yahweh is the proper object and the temple at Jerusalem the proper location. Second, they share Deuteronomy's concern for right leadership, addressing the issue in connection with the kings of Israel and Judah.

The consideration of these themes, however, is in a context in which temple and monarchy have disappeared. The two books of Kings, therefore, have (in common with some Psalms, especially Ps 89) the particular characteristic that they reflect on the meaning of the promises concerning David and Zion in the light of their apparent dereliction. Being under Deuteronomic influence, 1, 2 Kings know full well the possibility of the covenantal curse. Noth is wrong, however, to think that it proclaims only this, for the prayer of Solomon at the dedication of the temple holds out hope that the covenantal relationship between God and Israel may survive even this cataclysm (1Ki 8:46–53). The implicit call to repent is ubiquitous and also implies the possibility of a future.[59] As we have seen, however, there is no strand of 1, 2 Kings that imagines that the future lies along the path of a

---

[59]H. W. Wolff saw this as one of the central characteristics of DtH; see "Das Kerygma des deuteronomistischen Geschichtswerks," *ZAW* 73 (1961), 171–86; English translation in W. Brueggemann and H. Wolff, *The Vitality of the Old Testament Traditions* (Richmond, Va.: John Knox, 1975), 83-100.

restored monarchy. It is significant that the prayer of Solomon, the most articulate expression of hope for the future in the books, anticipates no such thing, not even a return to the land. The two books of Kings issue a call to repent and leave open the question how God might then respond in grace.[60]

THE DEUTERONOMIC HISTORY AND THE INDIVIDUAL BOOKS

Our investigation of modern approaches to DtH led us to an interpretation of 1, 2 Kings. This was inevitable, because these two books have had a central place in the debate about the larger corpus. The movement from a consideration of methodology to theological interpretation was also inevitable, because, as we saw, methods of analysis always imported theological assumptions. The focus on two books of Kings, however, has raised questions that we must now address.

Our main concern in the present study is with what constitutes "Deuteronomic" theology. It may be thought that an extended treatment of 1, 2 Kings is at best an oblique approach to the issue under discussion. However, it has taken us back to questions raised earlier in the present chapter, namely, to what extent is there a unity in the so-called Deuteronomic literature, and in what sense do its parts each have an individual character. It is significant for the direction of our study that our consideration of works that looked for continuities throughout Deuteronomy–2 Kings should lead us into an exposition of one particular component (1, 2 Kings). The obvious next question is whether the other books in the corpus have distinctive characteristics and interests, as well as some sort of link with the theology of Deuteronomy.

A first step toward an answer may be taken by a further

---

[60]See further my "Narrative and Meaning in the Books of Kings."

observation about the theologies of Deuteronomy and 1, 2 Kings. As I have shown elsewhere, these books differ in their expression of hope for the future.[61] Deuteronomy 30:1–10 looks forward to a return of the people to the land to which they would in due course be exiled. The books of 1, 2 Kings, though conversant with the passage in Deuteronomy,[62] ask only in the prayer of Solomon at the dedication of the temple (1Ki 8:46–53) that when the people repented, their captors might show them compassion. Nowhere do 1, 2 Kings express any other hope than this for an end of the captivity. This difference seems to me to be best explained by the setting of 1, 2 Kings precisely in that period when the full sense of loss was being experienced. These two books, then, are "Deuteronomic" in the sense that they dialogue between the Deuteronomic tradition and the contemporary situation. Is this true of the other books also?

This question, of course, is too large for proper consideration in a study of the present size. However, it is important to try to sketch a possible answer.

Deuteronomic Theology and the Book of Joshua

Interpretation of the book of Joshua is widely based on the premise that more or less early material has been incorporated into a later, Deuteronomistic framework, that reinterprets it for its own time. Noth believed that a series of separate aetiological stories was combined into a coherent whole prior to the work of the Deuteronomist (Dtr) in the exile, whose main contribution was to add an introduction (Jos 1) and an epilogue (Jos 23), as well as some other material (e.g., 8:30–35, which recalls Dt 27:2–8).[63] The aim of Dtr for Noth was to stress God's help for Israel in the

---

[61]See "1 Kings VIII 46-53 and the Deuteronomic Hope."
[62]I have argued for this observation in the same article.
[63]Noth, *The Deuteronomistic History*, 36–40.

conquest of the land. Though the idea of a complete conquest was already present in the earlier "Compiler's" work (Jos 11:16–20a), Dtr underlines the point by his own additions, especially 11:23b and the related story of Caleb's possession of Hebron (14:6–15a).[64] Joshua's closing address (ch. 23), warning the people against the gods and cults they will find in the land and threatening retribution, is Dtr's last word in this book.[65]

Following Noth, T. C. Butler interpreted Joshua in terms of an assimilation of old stories to a contemporary situation and in terms of a Holy War ideology. His approach is well illustrated by his analysis of the story of Rahab. Butler believed that the book of Joshua is essentially exilic and post-exilic in its orientation, concerned with questions that exercised the communities of those periods. Events in the Joshua narrative are thus paradigmatic for such issues, including the character of law, leadership, and land.[66] The story of Rahab, in Butler's view, was originally a story with folklore elements and the common theme of a woman who offers hospitality. At a later stage in its development, it served to show how Israel had entered the land. Finally, in the hands of Dtr, it was used to illustrate the concept of total conquest in Holy War terms, Rahab herself giving expression to this idea (2:9–11, cf. v. 24). The story has thus become a simple affirmation of Holy War ideology; this is what makes it "Deuteronomic."[67] Similarly, the story of the central shrine at Shiloh (Jos 22), with its power to unify the ancient tribes, becomes a lesson for the exilic and post-exilic communities that have to face divisions of a new kind (between those who returned from exile in Babylon and those who never went; cf. Ezra–Nehemiah).[68]

---

[64]Ibid., 38–39.

[65]Ibid., 39–40.

[66]T. C. Butler, *Joshua*, WBC (Waco, Texas: Word, 1983), xxiv-xxvi.

[67]Ibid., 31–32, 34–35.

[68]Ibid., 243–44.

The issue of what is "Deuteronomic" in Joshua, however, is not a simple one, and other successors of Noth have treated it somewhat differently. For Mayes what is Deuteronomic consists of four key concepts: Israel as a single whole; this one people in covenant with Yahweh; the people under one leader; Holy War as the means of obtaining the land.[69] So far, he is in line with Noth. But the theological picture of Joshua is not quite uniform; therefore, somewhat under the influence of Smend, Mayes sees two distinct Deuteronomistic editions, one of which, produced by the Deuteronomistic historian, depicts a complete conquest, while the other introduces a note of conditionality, not least in Joshua 23.[70] Mayes thus highlights a difficulty in Noth's rather triumphalist reading of Joshua, namely, that it does not correspond to his understanding of the general purpose of Dtr, i.e., to explain the fall of the Israelite and Judean kingdoms in terms of the people's historic sin. Noth has, in fact, done little justice to those passages in Joshua that qualify somewhat ominously the picture of total conquest—those referring to remaining Canaanite enclaves (e.g. 13:1ff.; 15:63; 16:10) and those hinting at the people's possible failure to keep the covenant (e.g., ch. 23; see v. 16; also ch. 24, especially vv. 19–20, which he assigned rather preemptorily to a post-Deuteronomistic source).[71]

The difficulty presented by Holy War and total conquest in Joshua for interpreting that book in the context of DtH is further highlighted by the contrast many have noted between Joshua's picture of entry to the land and that of Judges. With this contrast in mind, B. S. Childs spoke of "a unique theological perspective of the Deuteronomic editor" that comes to the fore in Joshua, namely, that total conquest came as a result of the people's obedience at the outset of the

---

[69] A. D. H. Mayes, *The Story of Israel from Settlement to Exile*, 41–43.

[70] Ibid., 46–49. This is in line with his understanding of the composition of Deuteronomy (for Smend, see analysis earlier in this chapter).

[71] Noth, *The Deuteronomistic History*, 8.

campaign in Canaan. The picture of slow, difficult acquisition of the land is thus relegated to Judges, marking the end of the ideal period of obedience.[72] Childs qualifies his idea of conflicting perspectives on the conquest by arguing that they have been purposefully built into the present chronological arrangement of material in Joshua–Judges. Nevertheless, the idea of a "unique" Deuteronomic perspective is inherently problematic for any coherent understanding of what "Deuteronomic" might mean.

The much vaunted conflict between Joshua and Judges is just one further aspect of the difficulty inherent in the view that Joshua essentially presents an ideology of Holy War. In our brief discussion we have seen hesitations over the meaning of Joshua and, by the same token, over what is "Deuteronomic" in it. These hesitations are reminiscent of those that we noted at an earlier stage of the argument in relation to Deuteronomy. Here as there they stem from a too ready commitment both to a theory of the composition of the book and to a view of its setting. The setting, however, remains variable enough (Josianic? exilic?) to allow for understandings of the book that are at odds with each other.

Some recent work on Joshua has challenged the Deuteronomistic theory in different ways. K. L. Younger's comparison of Joshua 9–12 with ancient Near Eastern conquest accounts has shown that the various elements that compose the biblical narrative in question are explicable in terms of the conventions of such accounts. Indeed, it is his thesis that these chapters have been deliberately modeled on such parallel narratives. He uses this as *prima facie* evidence for the unity of the narrative, which thus renders redundant the appeal to both aetiology (since alleged aetiological elements are often commonplaces of conquest narratives)[73] and multi-

---

[72]B. S. Childs, *Introduction to the Old Testament as Scripture* (London: SCM, 1979), 249–50.

[73]An example is the rolling of stones against the mouth of the cave at Makkedah (Jos 10:16), since the piling up of stones was common in

ple sources or editions.[74] Younger also calls into question other features thought to be characteristic of Dtr in Joshua. For example, the ideas of "all Israel" and of total conquest itself are explicable in terms of the hyperbole typical of all ancient conquest accounts.[75] His conclusion about dating is undogmatic; the "transmission-code" that he thinks Joshua 9–12 shares with other ancient narratives of similar type characterizes accounts known from as broadly defined a period as 1300–600 B.C.[76] This conclusion about the book's genre and about the composition of chs. 9–12 (extrapolated to the whole conquest account) allows for a complete reassessment of its date and purpose, and of course its relation to Deuteronomy and other Deuteronomic literature.

Younger's focus on the genre of the text has a point of contact with another kind of approach to Joshua—that which tries to understand it as a text in its entirety and in its own terms. R. Polzin's interpretation of Joshua is strikingly different at crucial points from those that derive from Noth's transmission-historical approach. It is true that Polzin is like the more conventional interpreters in that he uses the term "Deuteronomist," supposing that the audience of Joshua (as well as of Deuteronomy and Judges) is exilic,[77] and that the text as we have it embraces a number of "voices" that are in conflict with each other. Nevertheless, there is an underlying ideological tendency in the book, an "ultimate semantic authority,"[78] to which the "voices" have become subordinate. This approach allows a greater profundity to Joshua than one that begins from transmission-history, because all the ele-

---

warfare; K. L. Younger, *Ancient Conquest Accounts: A Study in Ancient Near Eastern and Biblical History Writing* (Sheffield: JSOT, 1990), 220–25.

[74]Ibid., 251–52.

[75]Ibid., 241–43, 248.

[76]Ibid., 263.

[77]R. Polzin, *Moses and the Deuteronomist*, 145.

[78]Ibid., 20–21. The term is borrowed from M. Bakhtin, *Problems of Dostoevsky's Poetics* (Ann Arbor: Ardis, 1973).

ments in the text belong in principle to the message that is articulated. There are no "relics" here.[79]

The dominant voice that Polzin finds in Joshua knows full well the tension between promise and threat that Mayes had explained in terms of Deuteronomistic editions. In fact, the discrepancy between the promise of land in the book and its fulfillment he believes is central to the ideology of Joshua.[80] He notes a correspondence between the imperfect realization of the promise and the imperfect obedience of the Israelites. The story is at heart a reflection on Israel's inability to take the land completely. His understanding of Dtr is thus strikingly different from Noth's univocal ideology of conquest.

Polzin's treatment of the Rahab narrative illustrates his method. Far from seeing this, as Butler did, as a triumphalist celebration of conquest in Holy War terms, he interprets it as an instance of the failure of Israel to be faithful to the terms on which the land is promised. The very act of sending spies he sees as a timid failure of faith, a deviation from the command of Deuteronomy 1:21 (cf. Jos 1:2, 9), and Joshua himself is guilty (2:1). The sparing of Rahab, furthermore, flouts the terms of the "ban" (Heb. *herem*; see Dt 7:1–5; 20:16–18).[81] The whole story is an extended reflection on Deuteronomy 9:4–5, in which Moses told Israel that they would enter the land, not because of their righteousness, but in spite of their stubbornness of heart. The Rahab story illustrates, therefore, a great irony that Polzin finds in Deuteronomy itself, namely, that Israel occupies a land she does not deserve. Her sin, however, has the consequence that she does so only imperfectly, and that correspondingly there continue to live in the land other nations who also do not "deserve" to be there (according to the terms of the ban), but

---

[79]I disagree with Mayes when he argues that Polzin's approach can coexist peacefully with conventional source and redaction criticism; Mayes, *The Story of Israel from Settlement to Exile*, 44.

[80]R. Polzin, *Moses and the Deuteronomist*, 80.

[81]Ibid., 85–86.

who are. Polzin thus sees the narrative not as a record of total conquest of the Canaanites, but as an explanation of why they are still there.

It is clear that this view is significantly different both from those that see the book of Joshua exhibiting an ideology of total conquest and Holy War (e.g., Noth), and from those that resolve tensions by postulating conflicting sources (e.g., Smend, Mayes). Polzin's Joshua has an ultimate unity of concept, within which the dialogue between different "voices" is part of the meaning of the text. The book is not a case of conflicting viewpoints in self-contradictory juxtaposition, whether conceived as law versus grace, or as threat challenging promise. Rather, the relationship between these polarities is the stuff of the reflection in the book.

The theses of Younger and Polzin are different, but constitute powerful challenges to the consensus about Dtr in Joshua. Each in its own way throws attention on to the book as a unity and shows that its various parts can be understood to contribute fruitfully to the whole. Neither is dogmatic about dating (despite Polzin's acceptance of critical orthodoxy on the point).[82] It is not possible, therefore, to draw firm conclusions about the function of Joshua in its setting on the basis of their studies. However, two concluding observations may be made: First, we may maintain a unity between form and meaning in Joshua. This means that there is no need to see unresolved tensions in the material; the book has a meaning. Second, we have seen that when we say "Deuteronomic," we mean something complex; if the book has a meaning, it will not be in terms of a simplified dogma of either law or grace; our Deuteronomist is neither a propagandist of the Holy War nor a sombre legalist.

The lineaments of an interpretation of the book have been outlined in our reading of Polzin. Younger's contribution is weaker on interpretation than on method. His

---

[82]Ibid., 18.

observation that the book has adopted the habits of expression of the conquest narrative as a genre need not lead to the conclusion that it also echoes its ideology. Certainly, part of Joshua's message is that Yahweh is supremely able to guarantee his promises and that therefore Israel need not fear.[83] However, Polzin has shown features of both Deuteronomy and Joshua that facilitate a more satisfying reading of the latter: Israel holds the land only by God's mercy, but loses it when the Israelites are unfaithful.

In what way, therefore, is Joshua in dialogue with the Deuteronomic tradition? Can a setting be proposed for it that makes most sense of its contents? As we saw, Younger's comparative study allowed for some flexibility on dating. In any case the book cannot be dated by means of formal characteristics alone, but also requires consideration of what is known of religious thought in Israel. It is at this point that certainty is elusive and that speculation takes over, sometimes dogmatically. We have seen in chapter 3 that attempts to date Deuteronomy (in the seventh century B.C.) suffered from lack of reliable criteria, and that interpretations of the book varied widely with different proposals as to precise settings. The same is true of Joshua. The exilic dating favored by Noth and adopted by Butler and others, including Polzin, depends more on the habit of mind cultivated by the theory of the exilic Deuteronomist than on data from the book itself. That theory lends a certain plausibility to the idea that Joshua should be read with exilic concerns in mind. However, the fact that a book can be shown to be relevant to a certain age does not require that it was composed then. The issues with which Joshua deals, such as leadership, faithfulness to the covenant, and possession of the land and the threat to it from non-Israelite peoples, would have been pressing at any time.

There are, indeed, some indications of a perspective in

---

[83]Younger, *Ancient Conquest Accounts*, 232–34.

Joshua that is at some distance from the events described, notably in the phrase "to this day" (4:9; 5:9; 6:25; 7:26; 8:28; 9:27). These notices do not identify a particular time in Israel's history, but a long time is scarcely required. The allusion to Rahab (see especially 6:25) is most easily comprehensible if the gap between the event and the comment is short. Furthermore, the association of the phrase in the notice about the Gibeonites (9:27) with "the place the LORD would choose," an allusion to the Deuteronomic provision for a place of worship (cf. Dt 12:5, etc.), is evidence of a date in the seventh century or later only in the context of a prior commitment to the view that that requirement is to be so dated.

The book of Joshua interacts significantly with the theology of Deuteronomy at the points of possession and distribution of the land, of covenant-renewal and the concern for faithfulness (e.g., Jos 8:30–35; 24), of the unity of the people, and of the reflection of this unity in the practice of worship. We have already discussed the former two themes, and they need no further comment. The latter two require elaboration.

The unity of Israel is one of the great themes of Deuteronomy.[84] It is reflected in Joshua in the picture of a single people entering the land under the leadership of one man, Joshua, the successor of Moses. Paradoxically, it appears also in relation to the division of the land, since that presupposes an idea of common inheritance and of cohesion. Perhaps an inverted affirmation of the brotherhood of Israelites also occurs in the relegation of the Gibeonites to the performance of menial tasks, a reflection of the Deuteronomic "double standard" regarding foreigners (e.g., Dt 15:3).

Most significantly, the unity of Israel is affirmed in the

---

[84]This was expounded by G. von Rad in *Das Gottesvolk* (Stuttgart: Kohlhammer, 1929), 49–58; see also McConville, *Law and Theology in Deuteronomy*, 19–20.

crisis involving the erection by Reuben, Gad, and the transjordanian half-tribe of Manasseh of an altar by the Jordan (Jos 22:9–34). This provoked the ire of their fellow-Israelites because it implicitly challenged the centrality and supremacy of Shiloh as the place of worship for all Israel, as well as the rights of Yahweh among his people (vv. 16–20). The "Deuteronomic" character of the issues here are beyond dispute. However, the fact that the "altar of the LORD" is at Shiloh, not Jerusalem, is hard to square with a definition of "Deuteronomic" in terms of the Josianic reforms that promoted worship in Jerusalem and aimed to suppress it elsewhere, especially in the northern territory. For this reason, it is hard to avoid the conclusion that at least a core of the present narrative belongs to a time before the period of the monarchy, when the centrality of Shiloh in Israel was in fact being asserted (cf. Jdg 21:21; 1Sa 1–3).[85]

The narrative, indeed, is intelligible only on such a view. The immediate issues facing the people are the unity of twelve-tribe Israel, the psychological problem posed by the Jordan to such unity, the importance of one place of worship as a symbol of the exclusive demands of Yahweh, the practical difficulty of any such place functioning as an all-Israel sanctuary for scattered groups, and the temptation to non-Yahwistic worship that would be mediated by the erection of other altars. It must be granted that some of these issues (e.g., the basic requirement of loyalty to Yahweh and its relation to a central sanctuary) can hardly be confined to the pre-monarchical period. However, the exilic theology found in 1, 2 Kings has different primary concerns from Joshua 22, as we have seen, namely, the judgment on both

---

[85]See K. Moehlenbrink, "Die Landnahmasagen des Buches Josua," *ZAW* 15 (1936), 236–68; Butler, *Joshua*, 243–44. J. A. Soggin's belief that the narrative in its present form is actually interested in the claims of Jerusalem has no support in the text itself, and is merely based on the dogma that Deuteronomic theology is Jerusalemite; see *Judges*, OTL (London: SCM, 1972), 214.

Israel and Judah and the question of a future for Judah beyond the exile. Its interest in Israel, furthermore, is couched in different terms: The transjordanian issue is now anachronistic, the division between north and south has come to the fore, and the northern kingdom indeed serves as a paradigm for the eventual fate of the southern (2Ki 17). While it is reasonable, therefore, to reflect on the ways in which the story in Joshua 22 might have become relevant to later generations,[86] there is no good reason to suppose that it is itself a product of Jerusalemite propaganda, whether Josianic, exilic, or even later. As Butler admits, "The Shiloh tradition may have exercised an important influence on the book of Joshua as a whole."[87] Joshua 22:8–34 suggests that this book is "Deuteronomic" in the sense that it applies Deuteronomic thinking in an early stage of Israel's history. Like the books of 1, 2 Kings, it interacts with the Deuteronomic tradition in a way that is appropriate to its time.

An innovative contribution to the interpretation of Joshua has been made by H. J. Koorevaar, who has analysed it into four main sections: (a) 1:1–5:12; (b) 5:13–12:24; (c) 13:1–21:45; (d) 22:1–22:33. These sections can be designated thematically as follows: (a) going over (*'āḇar*), (b) taking (*lāqaḥ*), (c) dividing (*ḥālaq*), d) worshiping (*'āḇad*). The themes are marked by leading words that, as can be seen from the Hebrew forms, correspond closely in an *a-b-b-a* pattern.[88] It is the third section, in Koorevaar's view, that

---

[86]Butler, *Joshua*, 243–44.

[87]Ibid., 243.

[88]H. J. Koorevaar, *De Opbouw van het Boek Jozua* (Heverlee: Centrum voor Bijbelse Vorming Belgie v. z. w., 1990), 283. Note that *lāqaḥ* and *ḥālaq* correspond in terms of a well-known phenomenon in Hebrew discourse, where the consonants of one word echo those of another, though they occur in a different order. As for *'āḇar* and *'āḇad* the Hebrew r and d are so close in form as to be capable of confusion with each other. Koorevaar's work is a doctoral thesis accepted by the Protestant Theological Faculty in the University of Brussels. It is published in Dutch with an English summary. References here are, for convenience, to the English summary.

yields the structural-theological purpose of the book. The structure of this section can be expressed as a concentric pattern, its center being 18:1–10, in which the Tent of Meeting is taken to Shiloh and the land is surveyed for occupation.[89] Because of this observation, Koorevaar regards 18:1 as a crucial point in the book: The setting up of the Tent of Meeting at Shiloh signals the bringing of the whole land under the control of Israel and the fulfillment of the promise that Yahweh would dwell among them there at a place that he would choose.[90]

Koorevaar draws from his observations a conclusion about dating that accords with the one just offered above on the basis of our consideration of Joshua 22, namely, that the prominence of Shiloh is hard to square with an origin of the book from a much later period than that sanctuary's demise. His detailed structural analysis lends weight to the extension of this claim to the whole book. His study therefore supports the contention that Joshua prosecutes "Deuteronomic" interests in a time and in terms that are peculiar to itself. We would only qualify his interpretation (as Younger's) in order to do justice, as Polzin tried to do, to the warnings in the text that counsel against seeing it as naively triumphalist.

---

[89]The division of the material is as follows (ibid., 289):

1. 13:8–33 Transjordan for 2 1/2 tribes;
2. 14:1–5 The principles of the division;
3. 14:6–15 Beginning: Caleb's inheritance;
4. 15:1–17:18 The lot for Judah and Joseph;
5. 18:1–10 The Tent of Meeting taken to Shiloh and the apportioning of the land;
6. 18:11–19:48 The lot for the seven remaining tribes;
7. 19:49–51 Ending: Joshua's inheritance;
8. 20:1–6 God's fourth initiative: designating cities of refuge;
9. 20:7–21:42 Cities of refuge and Levitical cities.

[90]Koorevaar finds this promise in Lev 26:11–12, ibid., 290; it might equally be found in Dt 12, of course.

Deuteronomic Theology in the Book of Judges

Like the book of Joshua, Judges has widely been regarded as a Deuteronomistic compilation of earlier material. Noth thought that Dtr had at his disposal a tradition of legendary "heroes," already in a connected narrative, with which he combined a different tradition of "minor judges" (found in Jdg 10:1–5; 12:7–15). These he connected by means of passages composed by himself, in a process that made the legendary heroes into "judges" (by analogy with the minor figures; cf. 2:16, 18).[91] He further provided a general introduction to the whole period.[92] The prologue and epilogue to the book as we have it are post-Deuteronomistic, their alleged pro-monarchical stance being at odds with Dtr's own hostility to the monarchy. The epilogue, indeed, is a false ending of the book, interrupting Dtr's account of the period as he had conceived it, for its true ending in Noth's view was 1 Samuel 12.[93] Dtr for his part, though he charted an intensification in Israel's tendency to apostasy in the period,[94] nevertheless saw the system of charismatic judges as more in accordance with true Yahwism; his account was therefore designed to show how they were able, with God's help, to deliver the people from their various tormentors.[95]

By such an account, Noth has again attempted to explain what he sees as the diverse material within a single book of DtH. The book of Judges promotes a certain model of leadership within Israel, whose rejection, in the demand for a king (1Sa 8), was ominous for the future.[96] The theory has problems that Noth answers in various ways. First, as we

---

[91]Noth, *The Deuteronomistic History*, 43–44.
[92]For Noth this is 2:6–3:6; ibid., 7–8, 42. Mayes, however, defines it as 2:11–3:6; see *Judges*, OT Guides (Sheffield: JSOT, 1985), 31–32.
[93]Noth, *The Deuteronomistic History*, 8, 121, cf. 5; see also Mayes, *Judges*, 13–16.
[94]Noth, *The Deuteronomistic History*, 46.
[95]Ibid., 49.
[96]Ibid.

have seen, parts of the book that appear actually to promote the monarchy (Jdg 17–21) are not considered Deuteronomistic. Second, Noth is obliged, by the deficiencies of some of the judges themselves, to maintain a distinction between the institution of judge and the person. Thus Gideon, who leads the people astray in the matter of the idolatrous ephod that he builds at Ophrah (8:24–27), does not, according to Noth, take part in this cult himself, but "as a savior appointed by God, prevented the worst from happening and thus made possible the forty years of 'rest' which continued as long as he was alive."[97] There is a tension here that calls into question the idea that the office of judge gains unqualified approval from Dtr. Third, a difficulty attaches to the idea of a Dtr who was so enthusiastic about a judicial system that was long defunct in his (exilic) time.

Others, perhaps sensitive to this last problem, have tried to give to Dtr's handling of the material in Judges a more contemporary edge. Smend's DtrN, for example, focuses on the theme of foreign peoples remaining in the land after the occupation as a pressing issue in his own day. Ancient Israel's inability to possess the land completely thus becomes a paradigm of the exiles' deprivation of it and thus teaches them the importance of covenant faithfulness.[98] This may provide Judges with a more plausible purpose in an exilic setting than Noth could find. However, Smend's general analysis is open to question, as we have seen,[99] and the interpretation of Judges through exilic eyes owes more to the theory of extensive Deuteronomistic activity in that period than to clear evidence from the book itself.

As in the case of Joshua, the Deuteronomistic theory regarding Judges as outlined above has received serious criticism in recent studies. Both B. G. Webb and L. R. Klein

---

[97]Ibid., 46.
[98]Smend, "Das Gesetz und die Völker," 506–8.
[99]See earlier in this chapter.

have interpreted the book as a coherent whole, in which distinctions between early and late material, between ancient story and editorial framework, retreat behind demonstrations of narrative art. Webb sees Judges 1:1–3:6 as the proper introduction to the book, establishing the theme of the whole composition, i.e., the question why the Canaanites were not completely driven out of the land.[100] Similarly, the so-called "epilogue" (chs. 17–21) is integral to the unfolding narrative, making specific links with elements in its main part (3:7–16:31).[101] Furthermore, the prologue and epilogue are not accurately characterized as pro-monarchical in contrast to a more dominant anti-monarchical tendency in the book. The issue of the mode of leadership is not of central concern in itself, and the intimations of monarchy in chs. 17–21 serve the needs of narrative "closure" more than of ideology.[102]

As Webb and Klein view the book, tensions in the subject-matter, rather than betraying the presence of different sources or editions, are part of its meaning. Webb understands the introduction to the book as setting the scene for it in terms of an ironic tension between possession, yet non-possession, of the land. Klein, as the title of her study shows, also sees deep irony in the book, deriving from two different perceptions of reality—that of Yahweh and that of Israel. According to the former, the land is a gift of Yahweh that Israel is simply called to accept as such; according to the latter, the land must be taken by human device. However, where Yahweh's perception is knowing, Israel's is ignorant. The irony of the book, prepared for in the introduction, lies in the counterpoint of these two perceptions. The tragedy is that Israel's very obsession with the details of conquest and possession corresponds to a deviation from faithful Yahwism, whose consequence is nothing less than failure to possess.[103]

[100]Webb, *Judges*, 116.
[101]Ibid., 197–201.
[102]Ibid., 200.
[103]Lillian R. Klein, *The Triumph of Irony in the Book of Judges* (Sheffield: Sheffield Academic Press, 1988), 23–24, 35–36.

The individual stories exhibit the basic tensions that are thus introduced. Ehud, the left-handed man, defeats the Moabite tyrant Eglon by means of an unworthy deception.[104] Gideon is not content with a victory achieved with God's help, but pursues in addition a private vendetta.[105] Jephthah, by his fateful vow, attempts to make victory more secure, though it is in any case assured because the Spirit of Yahweh is with him.[106] And Samson, in the blindness that is the consequence of his self-indulgent dallying with Philistine women (implying foreign religion), symbolizes an Israel that will bring death upon itself.[107] For both Webb and Klein the degeneration from the early figures to the later is an essential part of the portrayal; the epilogue is thus a fitting conclusion to the narrative, for it pictures social and religious chaos and describes the loss of the land (such as the highly suggestive northern migration of the Danites, as if they are on their way *out of* the land [ch. 18], and the ominous allusion to Shiloh "in Canaan" [21:12]).

The extent to which this kind of treatment of the text presents a challenge to the more traditional critical approach emerges from a closer look at one example, Webb's interpretation of the Jephthah narrative. For contrast, Mayes' analysis of the story may first be noted. In his view, the basic story of Jephthah is contained in 11:1–11, 29–33, to which have been added a long interpolation concerning Israel and Moab (11:12–28), an explanation of a ceremonial mourning rite (11:34–40), and a composite legendary account dealing with relations between Gilead and Ephraim (12:1–6). After these had been brought together to form an early version of the Jephthah story, 10:6–16 was prefixed as part of that

---

[104]Ibid., 37–39; Webb, *Judges*, 128–32.

[105]Webb, *Judges*, 151.

[106]Ibid., 62–65.

[107]Ibid., 172; cf. Klein, *The Triumph of Irony*, 137.

Deuteronomistic editing, giving the central part of the book of Judges its present shape.[108]

Webb, on the other hand, considers the whole section 10:6–12:7 as a narrative, composed of five episodes, that comprises a coherent literary unit at the levels of subject-matter, plot, characterization, and theme.[109] The first episode is 10:6–16. Unlike Mayes, Webb sees this not as a mere afterthought to the main narrative, but as a careful preparation of its theme. Verse 16 does not, as is sometimes thought, resolve the issue of Israel's apostasy with Yahweh's acceptance of her repentance. Rather, it expresses his impatience at the calculating nature of the "repentance" offered, which he now knows as a characteristic ploy. With this unresolved tension, the stage is set for further scenes in which words belie real intentions. In Episode 2 (10:18–11:11), the Gileadites' appeal to Jephthah to be their leader involves a calculation that parallels the Israelites' false repentance, and their acceptance of him as their "head and commander" (11:11) corresponds in turn to Israel's acknowledgement of Yahweh in 10:16a.[110] Moreover, Jephthah himself is guilty of duplicity in his language, concealing personal ambition behind a cloak of piety. In relation both to the Gileadites and to the Ammonites (11:12–28, Episode 3), Webb argues that Jephthah is really pursuing his own interests.[111] Finally, in Episode 4 (11:29–40), the infamous vow is a triumph of ambitious calculation over faith, with tragic and ironic consequences. This conclusion, incidentally, is partly based on a comparison of 11:29–32 with the account of Othniel in 3:10; it shows that the coming of the Spirit of Yahweh is sufficient guarantee of victory. The tragic irony of the vow with its consequences lies in its redundancy and springs from

---

[108]Mayes, *Judges*, 28–29, 33.

[109]Webb, *Judges*, 76.

[110]Ibid., 51–54.

[111]Ibid., 52, 57–60.

lack of faith.[112] The final episode (12:1–7) shows a Jephthah who has had the potential to be great and to give Israel honorable leadership, but who has been reduced to domestic squabbling with the Ephraimites.

The meaning of the Jephthah story, therefore, is in terms of a debasement of religion to the level of politics. Jephthah, who has allowed cunning ambition to dominate his relationship with Yahweh, is like Israel, whose "repentance" is also calculating. Yahweh's attitude, furthermore, cannot be simply summed up in a rewards and punishment schema, but reflects a deep personal and emotional involvement with Israel. The Lord intervenes to save Israel from Ammon. But as regards Jephthah, "he never really approves of him. His silence is the other side of his anger."[113]

Here as in Joshua, therefore, treatments of the text that pay close attention to narrative technique produce a significantly different interpretation from those that understand the Deuteronomic endeavor in terms of Josianic reform or exilic afterthought. Attempts to explain the text in terms of self-contradictory editorial accumulation are shown to be inadequate as the reader discovers far more profound conflicts that constitute the meaning of the narrative itself, and that are deliberately achieved with great artistry for a theological purpose. Especially interesting in Webb's interpretation is the close interconnection between what is elsewhere regarded as Deuteronomistic introduction or framework and the core of the story. It is also significant that his treatment produces a more subtle understanding of the theology of the narrative than standard interpretations of Deuteronomic theology.

---

[112]Ibid., 60–65.
[113]Ibid., 74–75.

Dating Judges

As with Joshua the question of dating is closely connected with interpretation. In what setting does the portrayal of Israel in Judges make most sense? We have expressed doubts about finding a key in divergent attitudes toward the monarchy[114] and suggested that there is no compelling reason, intrinsic to Judges, for ascribing it to a Josianic or exilic setting. One passage that is often taken as a clue to the book's perspective is 18:30, which says that the image that the Danites brought with them on their migration north, along with the priest of Micah who had accompanied them (vv. 18–20), and that they set up following their re-settlement in Dan, remained "until the time of the captivity of the land." This captivity is often identified in connection wth the Assyrian incursions into the northern kingdom of Israel that began in the 730s and culminated in 722 B.C.[115] The perspective of the book of Judges would thus be fixed in the period after the fall of the north and would fit well with the view that it was Josianic.

This interpretation of the phrase in question is by no means certain, however. The Danites may have had a tenuous hold on their new territory, as is suggested by the tendency of the narrative itself,[116] and this situation may have been reflected in some loss of it, perhaps temporary, of which we have no record. That the text is referring to some event close to those that are narrated in the context is suggested by the parallel information in the next verse (v. 31), that the

---

[114]As in Noth's and Mayes' assessment of the prologue and epilogue; see above, nn. 92–93. Doubts about a pro-monarchical orientation of the closing chapters of Judges (17–21) have also been expressed: W. J. Dumbrell, " 'In those days there was no king in Israel; every man did what was right in his own eyes.' The Purpose of the Book of Judges Reconsidered," *JSOT* 25 (1983), 23–33.

[115]Soggin, *Judges*, 277–78.

[116]As expounded by Webb, *Judges*, 184–88; cf. Klein, *The Triumph of Irony*, 159.

image remained until the fall of the sanctuary at Shiloh. We have observed that Shiloh plays an important role in the narrative of Joshua, the setting up of the sanctuary there being a culminating point in the story of the possession of the land (Jos 18:1).[117] Judges 18:31 is thus an echo of Joshua 18:1, intimating the loosening hold of Israel on the land (cf. the note that is also struck in relation to Shiloh at Jdg 21:12). Given the importance of Shiloh in the narrative, both here and in Joshua, "the captivity of the land" referred to in v. 30 is most naturally understood in relation to its fall, the historical context of this event being the Philistine ascendancy prior to the time of Saul.

In this way the subject-matter and theme of Judges can consistently be seen against the background of the period from which the stories are derived. The issues are the tenure of the land that is jeopardized by unfaithfulness to the covenant, the cohesion of the people (e.g., in Deborah's song, Jdg 4), and the problems posed by a decentralized, charismatic style of leadership—in itself consistent with the ideal of Yahweh's kingship (propounded in Jdg 8:23; 9)—when the Israelites follow their own counsels in matters of religion. Judges is thus in a real sense a prelude to the period of monarchy, not that any part of it advocates monarchy in principle, but sees it as the inevitable next step. These are issues that may readily be understood against the background of the period just before the accession of Saul, and are once again in dialogue with the theological concerns that may be called Deuteronomic. It is worth saying again that the reflection on these issues is neither shallow nor jejune, but shot through with the ironic recognition that Israel's self-interested attempts to secure the blessings of the covenant for herself are the surest guarantee of their loss.

---

[117]See above, in the present chapter.

Deuteronomic Theology in the Books of 1, 2 Samuel

The books of 1, 2 Samuel, according to Noth, were composed from various traditions that already lay before the Deuteronomist and that he connected into their present form, though some of the connections had in fact already been made, arising naturally out of the subject-matter.[118] The older traditions, as described by Mayes, are: the birth of Samuel (1Sa 1:1–4:1a); the story of the ark (4:1b–7:1; 2Sa 6); the rise of Saul (1Sa 7:2–15:35); the rise of David (1Sa 16:1–2Sa 5:25); the Succession Narrative (2Sa 9–20; 1Ki 1–2), and an appendix (2Sa 21–24).[119]

Dtr's additions to these complexes are few and not extensive, because, according to Noth, the sources effectively articulated his concerns. Thus, Dtr's hostility to the monarchy, evident from 1 Samuel 8–12, is justified by the story itself, which tells of the failure and demise of Saul.[120] The story of the rise of David serves Dtr's purpose of presenting David as the model king by whom all subsequent kings must be judged (2Sa 8:15–18; cf. 1Sa 13:14),[121] even though, as events would show, he was to be the only one who would fulfill that ideal. The recovery of the ark (2Sa 6) was important for Dtr as a prelude to the building of the temple in Jerusalem, and therefore it fit well into his account of David's accession.[122] It is unclear how Noth thought the so-called Succession Narrative (SN), with its account of David's adultery and the revolt of his son Absalom, furthered Dtr's purposes.

Noth's understanding of Dtr in 1, 2 Samuel encounters problems that have been well recognized. The first concerns the portrayal of the monarchy. As we have noted, Noth found

---

[118]Noth, *The Deuteronomistic History*, 54.

[119]Mayes, *The Story of Israel from Settlement to Exile*, 83.

[120]Noth, *The Deuteronomistic History*, 54.

[121]Ibid., 54, 56; cf. Mayes, *The Story of Israel from Settlement to Exile*, 104.

[122]Noth, *The Deuteronomistic History*, 55.

Dtr's attitude to this institution in 1 Samuel 8–12, where he saw hostility to it because it arose out of the people's rejection of Yahweh as king (1Sa 8:7; 12:17). The question naturally arises how Dtr could take such a positive view of David. Noth thought that Nathan's prophecy itself (2Sa 7:8–16), the programmatic statement of God's commitment to the Davidic dynasty, pre-dated Dtr, on the grounds that neither the prohibition of the building of the temple nor the strong emphasis on the monarchy was in keeping with his thinking.[123] However, Noth suggested that Dtr both left this text in the narrative and actually made of David a model king. Mayes, who believes that Dtr's hand is evident in 2 Samuel 7, especially in the idea of the permanency of David's monarchy, notes that his attitude to it there "marks something of a change compared with earlier expressions on the subject in 1 Samuel 8–12."[124] He solves the difficulty by supposing that the opposition to the monarchy in that text was not directed against the institution as such, but only against the kingship of Saul in particular.[125] However, for Mayes this solution is not complete, because he does find hostility to the institution of kingship in principle in 1 Samuel 12. He therefore ascribes this passage to the second, anti-monarchical Deuteronomistic edition, for which he found evidence also in Deuteronomy–Judges.[126]

1 Samuel 8–12 itself, of course, poses a similar question: Why did Dtr, with his hostility to the monarchy (whether in principle or not), include traditions favorable to it within the pericope (according to Wellhausen's older literary-critical analysis of it accepted by Noth)?[127] One proposed solution, adopted by Mayes following Crüsemann, is that the debate

---

[123]Ibid.

[124]Mayes, *The Story of Israel from Settlement to Exile*, 104.

[125]Ibid.

[126]Ibid., 105.

[127]Noth, *The Deuteronomistic History*, 53, 124; cf. Mayes, *The Story of Israel from Settlement to Exile*, 86–87.

between pro- and anti-monarchical points of view had already been incorporated in the tradition that lay before Dtr, and that it had originated in the period between David's accession and the division of the kingdom.[128] This may in itself be a plausible answer to the particular historical-critical question about the origins of 1 Samuel 8–12; its validity in the context of 1, 2 Samuel as a whole, however, remains to be considered.

The view of 1, 2 Samuel thus proposed is that Dtr found sources that more or less enhanced his basic thesis and therefore suited his requirements. But parts of the material (the "pro-monarchical" sections of 2Sa 8–12) did not in themselves conform to his views, but they were allowed to remain in the text because they had, as it were, lost the argument; other parts could not be attributed to Dtr (according to Mayes) because they were incompatible with his ideology (2Sa 12). The basic tension between the hostility to monarchy in 1 Samuel 8–12 and the perceived promotion of David in 2 Samuel 7 and elsewhere is barely resolved by this hypothesis. Von Rad took issue with Noth by contending that DtH had incorported into its theology of history Messianic hopes—chiefly exemplified by 2 Samuel 7—that were circulating in the exilic period. He found, moreover, a hint of promise in the release of King Jehoiachin from his Babylonian incarceration to a place of honor at the king's table (2Ki 25:27–30).[129] Furthermore, according to von Rad, Noth did not account for the criticism of David implied in the narrative of his adultery, with its consequences for the instability of the state in SN.

The classical Deuteronomistic theory therefore presents significant problems when applied to 1, 2 Samuel. Those problems prompt the questions whether the separate tradi-

---

[128]Mayes, *The Story of Israel from Settlement to Exile*, 93–96; cf. F. Crüsemann, *Der Widerstand gegen das Königtum*; cf. R. P. Gordon, *1 and 2 Samuel: A Commentary* (Exeter: Paternoster, 1986), 27.

[129]G. von Rad, *Studies in Deuteronomy*, 74–91.

tion complexes in the books might not have an inherently closer relationship together than Noth thought, and whether these together might not in turn contribute more coherently to the meaning of the books as a whole. We may begin to answer these questions with reference to the stories of the rise of Saul and of SN.

Regarding 1 Samuel 8–12, the issue of its final orientation is not in doubt; it is clearly, as a unit, intended to show that the people's demand for a king was an act of disobedience to Yahweh. What is of interest is the nature of the narrative itself, for an understanding of it may throw light on the character and purpose of 1, 2 Samuel.

The traditional critical view that these chapters are a composite of passages that took opposing views about the monarchy has come under attack from a number of quarters. Some interpreters have recently attempted to read the pericope as a coherent unit, so that an appeal to conflicting sources becomes unnecessary.[130] Already E. M. Good saw an ironic progression within the chapters, according to which the people's enthusiasm for a king was transformed into chagrin because of the consequences of their demand; correspondingly, Saul's reluctance turned gradually to a self-confident arrogation of kingly prerogatives. The irony lies in this double arc that exhibits the failure of both people and king to be faithful to Yahweh.[131] In Good's treatment, the narrative is carefully composed, and all its elements function positively in it. Thus, the favorable impression of Saul at his introduction is not evidence of a "pro-monarchical" tendency, but rather highlights his natural qualities precisely as an ironic measure of his unsuitability and ultimate failure.

V. P. Long's more recent treatment also sees the passage as a carefully constructed reflection on the accession of Saul. In his view, the issue is whether Saul would accept the limits

---

[130]See R. P. Gordon, *1 and 2 Samuel* (1986), 26–30.

[131]E. M. Good, *Irony in the Old Testament* (London: SPCK, 1965), 59–66.

placed upon kingship within the Yahwistic theocracy. The passage does not reject kingship as such; rather it focuses on both the people's illegitimate request for a king and on Saul's inability to grasp the nature of the role that Yahweh permits him to take. This inability is exposed by his refusal, admittedly under pressure, to comply with the requirements of Samuel in 1 Samuel 8:7-8 (cf. 13:8-15).[132]

Finally, L. Eslinger has argued for the unity of 1 Samuel 1-12 as a story of twin crises in the covenant between Israel and Yahweh. The first arises because of the corrupt Elide priesthood at Shiloh and results in the defeat of Israel by the Philistines at Ebenezer. There Yahweh conspicuously refrains from coming to his people's aid and resists their belated attempt to coerce him to do so (1Sa 4:1-11). The terms used in 4:2, 10 for the defeat by the Philistines recall those of the covenantal curse of Deuteronomy 28:25.[133] The second crisis arises from the corrupt leadership of Samuel's own sons (8:1-3), which occasions the people's demand for a king. Yahweh's accession to this demand reveals a difference in intention between the people and himself. When they cry, "Long live the king!" (10:24), it turns out that the kingship is still theocratic (10:25), a surprise that Eslinger calls an "entrapment." When Israel accepts the terms in 11:15, it is a different outcome from that which they had originally sought; Saul is not, or rather, may not be, a "king like all the nations" (8:5). With the theocracy thus affirmed, furthermore, a resolution of *both* crises (in chs. 4 and 8) is achieved.[134]

These treatments, though they do not necessarily agree in all the details of interpretation, nevertheless mark a transition from the older critical approach to the text. In the modern studies, the subtleties and ambiguities contribute to

[132]V. P. Long, *The Reign and Rejection of King Saul*, 236-39.

[133]L. Eslinger, *The Kingship of God in Crisis*, 56-57.

[134]Ibid., 58-62. With Eslinger's understanding of 1Sa 1-12 against a covenantal background, cf. J. R. Vannoy, *Covenant Renewal at Gilgal* (Easton, Pa.: Mack Publishing Co., 1978).

the meaning. They show that there is here no mere interweaving of contrary tracts, for the truth about the arrival of a king on the Israelite stage is a greyer thing than that view realized. Even the parts of the narrative that put Saul in a good light have their dark hints about the events that are being set in train.[135] And the conclusion of the covenant in 11:15, followed by Samuel's ominous speech in ch. 12, is not the end of the story, but poses the question whether and how Israel may be faithful to their new tripartite covenant, involving Yahweh, the people, and the king. That question pervades the remainder of 1, 2 Samuel.

The question may be taken up again by a consideration of the reign of David and of SN in particular. The interpretation of the parts of the book in relation to the whole is raised at the outset by the question of the beginning of SN. For Rost the main part of the narrative began at 2 Samuel 9, but he saw the need to postulate some preparatory material because of the abrupt beginning there. He therefore suggested that the Michal episode (6:20–23) might have originally belonged with SN, and possibly also an original dynastic oracle (ch. 7).[136] The possibility that material in chs. 6 and 7 may have formed a prelude to SN has been received with greater or lesser enthusiasm by commentators,[137] though Gunn denied connections with any material in chs. 5–8 and found the beginning in chs. 2–4.[138]

Gunn rejected a connection between ch. 7 and SN on the grounds that they have clearly different themes. The dynastic oracle and its context are concerned with whether David shall have sons to sit on his throne at all, while SN asks *which* of his sons shall succeed. "Accordingly," he goes on, "the promise in ch. 7 which ensures David of a dynasty is simply irrelevant

---

[135]See D. M. Gunn, *The Fate of King Saul: An Interpretation of a Biblical Story* (Sheffield: JSOT, 1980), 62–65.

[136]L. Rost, *The Succession to the Throne of David*, 85–90.

[137]For bibliography, see Gunn, *The Story of King David*, 132, n. 6.

[138]Ibid., 63–76.

as a source of dramatic tension in the following stories about David and his sons."[139] The real antecedent of SN is the account of the death of Ishbosheth, ostensibly the last Saulide who might make a claim to the throne of Israel.[140]

Gunn's view invites criticism at two points. First, his clean separation of the themes of the dynastic oracle and SN is not convincing. Rather, they are complementary. The dynastic oracle resolves the question whether there will be a succession; the story of David and his household is then an ironic sequel, throwing a shadow over the promise. Second, it can no longer be assumed that 1 Kings 1–2 is the true ending of SN. It may be a natural sequel, but to see it as the true end of SN seems to me to narrow the concerns of the latter too much. On the contrary, the so-called Appendix to 1, 2 Samuel (2Sa 21–24) is almost certainly misrepresented by that name; rather than being an afterthought, these chapters are the true conclusion of 1, 2 Samuel.[141] When this is recognized, the story of David from 2 Samuel 9 on need not be seen only through the lens of "succession," but rather as a reflection on the Davidic kingship. The Appendix forms a concentric pattern: (a) 21:1–14; (b) 21:15–22; (c) 22:2–51; (c') 23:1–7; (b') 23:8–39; (a') 24:1–25),[142] which recapitulates the movement in 1, 2 Samuel from Saul to David, because of a correspondence in the roles of Saul and David in the elements (a) and (a'). This last narrative (ch. 24), in which the purchase of the threshing-floor of Araunah prepares for the building of the temple in 1 Kings, continues the story of the promise to David and contributes to its confirmation. The king's psalm (ch. 22) and his "last words" (23:1–7) also celebrate his establishment as king. Another note is sounded in the Appendix, however, interwoven with the motif of fulfillment. The movement from Saul to David is

[139]Ibid., 66–67.

[140]Ibid., 68.

[141]See references to Carlson and Brueggemann above, n. 14.

[142]Gordon, *1 and 2 Samuel* (1986), 45.

ominous, because the correspondence between the two, implicit in the structure of the Appendix, is not wholly explicable in terms of contrast. Rather there is a balancing of a famine in Israel attributable to a fault of Saul (a) with a plague on Israel attributable to David (a'). This latter feature also casts a shadow over the discovery of the threshing-floor of Araunah as the place where David is to erect his altar.

These points prompt further observations. It seems to me that Gunn has foreclosed the recognition of some of the connections and ironies that exist in the wider narrative of 1, 2 Samuel by his separation of SN from parts of its context. When the Appendix is viewed as the proper end of 2 Samuel, it helps towards a satisfactory interpretation of SN, for in both, questions are raised about whether the dynastic promise to David can really be the vehicle of permanent blessing for Israel. The darkening of expectation that charac- terizes the Appendix is in keeping with the sequence of the dynastic oracle and SN. The idea that SN was essentially the story that explained how David was succeeded by Solomon was never satisfactory, because it saw no function in the wider story for the failure of David and the crisis in both his own household and the state that ensued. Interpretations that have tried to understand these parts of Samuel in relation to each other have been more convincing.[143]

Furthermore, when SN is regarded as a kind of qual- ification of the dynastic oracle, the material in 2 Samuel can be more readily assimilated to the introduction of the issue of kingship in 1 Samuel 8–12. In the light of events in 2 Samuel, it is not accurate to say that the real problem in 1 Samuel 8–12 was the kingship of Saul as opposed to that of David. Rather, the subject of the books taken together is what happens when, in the fullness of time, Israel takes human

---

[143]See the interpretation of R. A. Carlson, who thinks that the stories of David's establishment of Jerusalem as the capital and worship-center show David under covenantal blessing, and that his adultery and civil war show him under the covenantal curse (*David: The Chosen King*, 23–25).

kingship into the covenantal scheme of things. Saul is not merely an unsatisfactory overture to the main program; the covenant, now involving a human king, continues to run a rough course, as it had done under the judges. In other words, no institution can guarantee Israel permanent salvation.

The reason for this lies in the disposition of Israel itself, whether in the people or in their representatives or in both. We have seen how unfaithfulness to the covenant manifested itself in the history of the judges, where the author posits an ironic counterpoint between Yahweh's perspective on events and that of the human personalities. Similar ironies are present in the stories of Saul and David, as we have seen already in the case of the former. As for the latter, Gunn has shown how an alternation between David as one who is willing to receive royal power from God and one who grasps at that power produces ambiguities of character and affects the course of events. Thus, when David is content both to receive status from God and to bestow it on others he is successful. Gunn finds this characteristic of David in 2 Samuel 2–5; 9; 10, in a certain personal restraint in the events leading up to his accession (chs. 2–5) and in his gift of land to Saul's son Mephibosheth (9:7). (He also finds it, incidentally, in 1Sa 24; 26, when David spares Saul). When he grasps at power in the Bathsheba story, in contrast, a chain of events is unleashed that results in the temporary loss of his kingdom. It is in turn a newly magnanimous David who receives the kingdom again (2Sa 15–18).[144]

An approach of this sort to 1, 2 Samuel suggests that what is at stake is not so much the advent of kings on the Israelite stage as the continuing story of the covenant between God and Israel. The substance of the story, it is true, is provided by the transition from judgeship to kingship, and from there to dynastic kingship—issues that were presum-

---

[144]Gunn, *The Story of King David*, 94–97 (see p. 95 for 1Sa 24; 26).

ably hotly contested in their day. The specific "Deutero-nomic" contours of the debate in 1, 2 Samuel, however, are drawn around the question whether Israel can be faithful to the covenant as it has been newly defined. In particular, can the king be content with a role within a theocratic framework? In 1, 2 Samuel we have the literary deposit of this debate (though, as we have seen, not in the sense of a simple interweaving of raw sources). It may be that we should allow the elapse of some time between the events recorded and the composition of the narrative.[145] Nevertheless, this need hardly amount to many generations.[146] Rather, 1, 2 Samuel, like Joshua and Judges before it, is its own particular expression of Deuteronomic theology. The issues raised here are hardly at home either in the exile (where the question of a properly theocratic king would be irrelevant) or in a hypothetical Josianic Dtr (since a celebration of the dynasty would not be served by the question marks set against it in 1, 2 Samuel).

It only remains to say, though the point should be clear already, that there are strong continuities between 1, 2 Samuel and the preceding books. The Deuteronomic theology forms, after all, a common bond. These continuities are in terms of the capacity of Israel to be faithful and of her persistent inability in this respect. An ironic contrast continues between Yahweh's perception of how Israel might enjoy the promised covenantal blessings and Israel's perception. These continuities emerge at times into the subject-matter itself. One example is the adumbration in Judges 6–9 of the issue of kingship, though in that place it remains a more or less marginal threat, while in 1, 2 Samuel it has

---

[145]Gunn points to the likely anachronism in 2Sa 12:20, where David goes into the "house of the LORD"—though the temple was not yet built; ibid., 32.

[146]Despite Gunn's contrary claim, ibid., 33. On his view that the language of "all Israel" is late and idealized (ibid.), see the treatment of Joshua, above, and the contention that this designation was entirely possible, even if hyperbolic, at an early stage of Israel's history.

become a reality.[147] The possibility of the loss of the land, furthermore, is always present. This gives a significance to intimations of exile that may extend beyond the immediate context of any one instance of it to provide new meanings in new times (cf. 1Sa 4:21–2 with Judg 18:30).[148]

Deuteronomic Theology in the Books of 1, 2 Kings

It is not necessary to dwell further on the Deuteronomic theology in 1, 2 Kings, since we discussed the subject earlier in this chapter. We noted there that the Deuteronomic idea in 1, 2 Kings was not uniform. It was widely held that there were two Deuteronomic editions of 1, 2 Kings, each of which took a different view of the future of the people and of the destiny of the monarchy, according to their different historical perspectives. We argued, in contrast, that 1, 2 Kings had a unified concept, and we demonstrated the delusiveness of the idea that salvation for the nation might be guaranteed by the institution of monarchy. This message was all too starkly borne out by the setting of 1, 2 Kings in the exilic period. These books, then, like the others we have discussed, interacted with Deuteronomic theology in their own way. We saw how their view of the future, by contrast with Deuteronomy 30:1–10, was influenced by their immediate setting.[149]

It will readily be seen that the view we have taken of 1, 2 Kings is compatible with that which we have taken of the other books in DtH. Instead of the jarring juxtaposition of contrary expectations (as in Cross's understanding of 1, 2 Kings), events and aspirations are portrayed with a strong

---

[147]This connection is noticed by D. Jobling in *The Sense of Biblical Narrative*, vol. 1 (Sheffield: JSOT, 1978). He sees Jdg 6–9 as a corrective anticipation of 1Sa 8–12. R. Polzin's opinion is to be preferred, however, when in a review of Jobling's book, he agrees that the Judges passage anticipates that in Samuel, but does not see it as corrective (*Biblica* 69 [1988], 123–25).

[148]Cf. Gordon, *1 and 2 Samuel* (1986), 97–98.

[149]See our analysis above; see also my article "1 Kings VIII 46-53 and the Deuteronomic Hope."

undercurrent of irony. Israel's dreams have no solid foundation when they are based on the pursuit of power. The ambiguities in the portrayal of Hezekiah (i.e., his appeasement of Assyria in 2Ki 19, and his pompous display before the Babylonian envoys in ch. 20) and of Josiah (i.e., his ill-judged march against Pharaoh Neco in 23:29–30) find resonances with those that we have found in the stories of Joshua, of the judges, and of Saul and David.

CONCLUSIONS: DEUTERONOMIC THEOLOGY IN JOSHUA–2 KINGS

A certain picture has been building up in our treatment of these books, both showing how they exhibit concerns expressed in Deuteronomy and yet revealing their individuality in doing so. Deuteronomy itself set a program before Israel and raised the question how the people of God might be able to put it into practice. They were, after all, by nature a "stiff-necked people," and it was not because of their righteousness but because of the wickedness of the other nations that they were to be given possession of the promised land (Dt 9:4–6). The ominous signs given in Deuteronomy (cf. 8:10–20, with its anticipation of the temptation to Israel to rely on her own strength, v. 17) lead finally to an acknowledgement there that the exile must take place before there can be a better-based relationship between God and Israel (30:1–10). The story in Joshua–2 Kings plays out what seem to be the inevitabilities highlighted in Deuteronomy. The story is always one of blessing that is forever within Israel's reach, yet never fully attained, and finally lost because of their failure to share Yahweh's perspective on him, themselves, and their history.

Our discussion of Joshua–2 Kings, and of Deuteronomy itself before them, has been the prerequisite of an attempted description of the essentials of "Deuteronomic Theology," the subject of the following chapter.

◆ 5 ◆

Deuteronomic Theology

W e have been building gradually towards a definition of Deuteronomic theology, seeking what is central or basic to that theology and recognizing that there may be room for somewhat different perspectives within its broad compass. Deuteronomy itself resisted the attempt to imprison it within one period or one narrowly defined set of interests. Its polarities (such as "law" and "grace") were not rival views vying to be heard, but rather belonged to its distinctive concept.

Deuteronomic theology, furthermore, could not be described in terms of Deuteronomy alone, but required the consideration of those books that bear an unmistakable relation to it and, as we have found, ventilate a variety of issues in its currents. The Deuteronomic achievement should not be underestimated; it is nothing less than a theology of God and Israel on the plan of the nation's entire history, from the promises made to Abraham to the restoration from exile. Remarkably, however, it does not develop its themes from the straitjacketed perspective of one period; attempts to understand the various books in question through the lenses of the time of Josiah or the exile were forced. Rather, the genius of the Deuteronomic corpus is that it has captured the particular lines of a succession of issues, all contemporary and urgent, without attempting to impose strict harmony.

We must now try to say what is the heart of the Deuteronomic concept. Our main difficulty in doing so lies in the deceptive profundity of the literature; in the attempt, we are at the point where the obvious gives way to the powerful and profound.

THE GOD OF ISRAEL

The God of Deuteronomy is first of all the only God, the One who alone is worthy of his people's allegiance (Dt 6:4). The discussion whether Deuteronomy is monotheistic in the strict sense is arid. The book always thinks of God's oneness in relational terms, that is, in the context of his relationship with Israel. It is this God, Yahweh, and not another, who is supreme in the affairs of Israel and of the nations—a point made in dialogue, explicitly and implicitly, with the polytheism of Canaan. The form of the book, evoking the ancient Near Eastern political treaty, is itself part of that dialogue. The affairs of Israel are not directed by kings, themselves in servitude to rival, unpredictable, and ultimately impotent gods. On the contrary, no one is king in Israel but Yahweh himself, as the Blessing of Moses proclaims (33:5). Furthermore, Yahweh's authority is not limited to the borders of his people's land. His capacity to deliver the Israelites from Egypt and to give them the land of Canaan is a function of his lordship over the entire world. This point too is made explicit in the book's finale, the Song of Moses, where the God Most High (*El Elyon*) fixes the boundaries of the nations, while Yahweh's special portion is Jacob (32:8). The point of this verse is to depict God first as the supreme God who governs nations and then as the one who has chosen Israel. The two names used for him are selected for their appropriateness and effect in the respective statements of that verse.[1]

It is against this background that DtH discusses the forms of human leadership. Deuteronomy itself limited royal powers severely, made submission to the commandments of Yahweh paramount (Dt 17:14–20), and advocated a diversified leadership (1:9–18). The demand for a king "such as all the other nations have" (1Sa 8:5) runs directly counter to this provision. The actual pursuit of oppressive policies by Israel's kings and their preference for foreign gods vindicated both the Deuteronomic view and Samuel's prophetic opposition to the people's demand. Judges, however, had hardly been more successful at stemming the tide of idolatry (Jdg 8:22–27).

GOD MADE KNOWN

Yahweh is not only supreme and unchallenged, but also knowable; his knowability is expressed in some of Deuteronomy's typical emphases. The theophany at Horeb occupies a prominent position in the book. Its portrayal there has particular traits. First, the author stresses the *words* spoken at the mountain and expresses reticence about the idea of a visible form of God (4:12, 33, 36). This strikes a markedly different note from the bold depiction of the theophany in Exodus 24:9–11. Although Deuteronomy 5:4 uses the words "the LORD spoke to you face to face," other statements in ch.

---

[1] I take Dt 32:8–9 to imply that Yahweh and the Most High are one and the same. The identification of Yahweh with the El who was known to the patriarchs is the point of the revelation of Yahweh's name to Moses (Ex 3:14; 6:2–3). *El Elyon* was one of the forms of that name (Gen 14:18). In its usage in the OT the name draws on the significance that it also had among Israel's neighbor nations, but only to claim that significance for Yahweh. On the present verse see P. C. Craigie, *The Book of Deuteronomy*, NICOT (Grand Rapids: Eerdmans, 1976), 379–80. Cf. F. M. Cross, *Canaanite Myth and Hebrew Epic* (Cambridge, Mass.: Harvard University Press, 1973), 44–75, for a discussion of the relationship between El and Yahweh in the OT.

5 obviously construe the encounter at Horeb in terms of speech. Whereas the wonder of the theophany in Exodus 24:9–11 is that human beings should see God and live, in Deuteronomy 5:24 it is that they should see God *speak with them* and live.[2]

Deuteronomy's reticence about the vision of God is part of a consistent tenet in OT theology that God should not be represented in visible or tangible form (Ex 20:4–5; Dt 5:8; cf. 4:15–16). The same concern underlies Deuteronomy's severe hostility to all idolatrous religions (Dt 13), characterized as they are by a materialist concept of God (or at least the danger of it). For this reason Deuteronomy takes great pains to show that God, although "dwelling" in his chosen santuary, does not do so in any way that diminishes his spirituality or freedom. The chief means of making the point is by the oft-repeated statement that he makes the chosen sanctuary "a dwelling for his Name" (12:11; 14:23; 16:2). Deuteronomy's related doctrines of a spoken revelation and the essential spirituality of God, therefore, are characteristic of its portrayal of God's presence among his people.

These ideas have further implications. The *spokenness* of the revelation at Horeb ensures that that event is not trapped back in the past. Rather, it is present anew in every generation. The point is starkly put in Deuteronomy 5:3, where the Horeb covenant is said to have been made not with the generation that actually experienced the theophany (i.e., the previous generation to the one addressed by Moses in Deuteronomy, the one that had perished during the forty years of wanderings in the desert, Nu 14:20–35), but with the new one, the legatees of the promise, who now stand expectant on the plains of Moab, ready to enter upon their

---

[2]Ex 24:9–11 is one of several passages reflecting the fear that seeing God must have fatal consequences: cf. Jdg 13:22; Isa 6:5. In all these passages the fear proves unjustified, because God's self-revelation is intended for salvation. Deuteronomy makes a similar point, putting it in a particular light because of its concern for God's spoken revelation.

inheritance. It is for this reason that Deuteronomy stresses the need to hear God's word "this day" (Dt 4:8; 5:1; 6:6; 7:11; 8:1, 11). For this reason too the need to teach the words of God to each succeeding generation is of paramount importance (4:9; 6:1–9). It is no accident that the best-known words in Deuteronomy among both Christians and Jews, the so-called Shema (6:4–5), are in the context of an instruction that has precisely this aim.

Since the revelation of God is new in every generation, it is not surprising that together with its manner, revelation continues to be a major theme in DtH. This theme appears in several ways. First, periodic exhortations and covenant renewals commit the people afresh to submission to Yahweh's commandments (Jos 1:7; 23:6; 1Sa 12:14–15; 2Ki 22:8; 23:1–3; cf. Jos 24:25–6; 2Sa 7:21).[3] Second, as the words of Deuteronomy were spoken by the prophet Moses, so did prophets continue to confront kings and people with the word of God. Elijah began his ministry when "the word of the LORD" came to him (1Ki 17:1). He accused the people on Carmel of having "abandoned the LORD's commands" (1Ki 18:18). That whole confrontation can be seen as the triumph of Yahweh's true prophet (like Moses, cf. Dt 18:14–20) over the false prophets of Jezebel's Baal. They espoused that blasphemous creed that God might be known by all manner of esoteric manipulation (Dt 18:10–11); for the true prophet, in contrast, God is known only by the hearing of his word. Finally, Elijah's encounter with the Lord on Horeb strongly recalls Moses' hearing of the word of God there (1Ki 19:9b–18). Other prophets—such as Micaiah, Elisha, Nathan, and

<hr>

[3]Despite manuscript evidence for "your servant" in 2Sa 7:21 (see P. K. McCarter, *II Samuel*, AB [New York: Doubleday, 1984], 234), "your word" is defensible in the light of the theology of the whole chapter as a fulfillment of the Deuteronomic promise (2Sa 7:1; cf. Dt 12:9) and of the Deuteronomic tone of David's prayer. The promise to David gains a kind of guarantee because of the known faithfulness of Yahweh to his word.

Huldah—likewise play important parts in the chastening of kings and in the announcement of God's purposes.

Finally, the theology of God's spirituality, the other side of his revelation by the word, is at the heart of his conflict with idolatrous religion throughout DtH. We see this in God's reluctance to accept that a "house" should be built as his dwelling, since such a thing can imply an attempt to control him (2Sa 7:5–7).[4] The point is resumed, paradoxically, in Solomon's prayer at the dedication of the temple, when he strives to guard the freedom and spirituality of God by means of the so-called "name-theology." Solomon asserts that God is not confined within the "house"; rather, heaven is his dwelling place, and the temple is merely the place where his "Name" dwells and is consequently a place of prayer (1Ki 8:27–30).

GOD MADE KNOWN IN HISTORY

The historical character of OT theology is well-known, but its significance requires elaboration. At one time it could be held that what distinguished Israel from its neighbors was a historical consciousness, a concept of linear history. Scholars claimed that the ideas of other nations were bound up so much with the annual seasonal rhythms that their gods were seen as nature gods, in stark contrast with Yahweh, the God of history.[5] Recent studies have shown that this polarization is untenable. In a much-cited work, B. Albrektson has shown that the gods of the ancient Near East were also thought to act "in history," in the sense that they gave victories in battle, and could be called on to give blessings or send curses on other nations; the Hittite treaties afford an

---

[4]See R. E. Clements, *God and Temple* (Oxford: Blackwell, 1965), for an exposition of the significance of temples in Canaanite religion.

[5]M. Noth, "The Understanding of History in Old Testament Apocalyptic," in *The Laws in the Pentateuch and Other Studies* (London: SCM, 1966; German 1954), 194–95.

excellent example of this belief.[6] Central biblical ideas such as God giving enemies "into the hands of" his people are replicated in non-Israelite inscriptions, and human kings are regarded as the executors of the god's will on earth.[7] By comparing the OT with ancient Near Eastern documents, Albrektson even questioned how far it has a distinctive idea of a "divine plan" in history, arguing that the idea of an over-arching scheme, usually associated with "salvation-history" approaches to OT theology, was not evident in the OT (with the exception of apocalyptic, which was untypical and may even have been influenced by Mesopotamia!).[8] Furthermore, the theological interpretation of events and the idea of a moral order, far from being new with SN (as von Rad had argued), was widespread throughout the ancient world and well-rooted in its religion.[9]

Albrektson tends to argue, therefore, that the OT cannot claim to be distinctive on the sole grounds of a sense of history. Uniqueness in its historical understanding can only be defended on the grounds of certain aspects of its religion. Albrektson himself admits that the idea of a "divine plan" must be different in the context of a monotheistic faith than in a polytheistic setting.[10] This is crucial to understanding the OT's view of history. Since Wellhausen, the distinctive contribution of the OT to the development of religion has often been found in "ethical monotheism," allegedly the discovery of the prophets of Israel.

E. W. Nicholson has recently revived this idea, contending that the decisive turning-point in Israel's thinking came

---

[6]B. Albrektson, *History and the Gods* (Lund: Gleerup, 1967), 17–21.

[7]Ibid., 38, 42–52.

[8]Ibid., 68ff. Albrektson here opposes J. Lindblom (*Prophecy in Ancient Israel* [Oxford, Blackwell, 1962], 325), who argued that the prophets believed in a divine plan for all of history.

[9]Albrektson, *History and the Gods*, 100ff. Cf. G. von Rad, *Old Testament Theology* (London and Edinburgh: Oliver and Boyd, 1962, 1965), 2.52, 308–17.

[10]Albrektson, *History and the Gods*, 96.

with the struggle for allegiance to Yahweh alone, whose traces survive in the Elijah-cycle.[11] In the covenantal demand for this type of exclusive allegiance lies that which marks out OT religion, for it implies a break with the determinism of contemporary religions, and offering in its place the freedom, responsibility, and open future that come from the belief in one God who is at once omnipotent, holy, and disposed to bless. This entails, of course, the capacity to criticize any power or institution that happens to have the ascendancy at any time. Our earlier argument that Deuteronomy was not conceived as an apologia for monarchy and Jerusalem cult, together with our claim throughout that neither Deuteronomy nor DtH should be seen as organs of Josiah's reform, obviously relate directly to this point.[12] For it is to Deuteronomy, I believe, that we should look in the first instance for the fullest exposition of the "revolutionary" ideas that mark Israel off from their neighbors, and in which their idea of history plays a crucial role.

The idea of history in Deuteronomy is so foundational that one can hardly discuss it without leading directly into the other topics in the book's theology (such as election and covenant). Even the ideas already mentioned (the supremacy and knowability of Yahweh) are obviously incomprehensible without it. However, the immediate entailments of Deuteronomy's theology of history are as follows. First, it implies the possibility of a personal relationship between Yahweh (one and omnipotent) and the human race, within which each is a responsible agent making free choices. This is everywhere assumed in the book rather than spelled out explicitly. Yet its uniqueness in the ancient world deserves mention in itself. People may not only know God, but can enter freely into

---

[11]E. W. Nicholson, *God and His People* (Oxford: Clarendon, 1986), 192–201.

[12]See our discussion in the previous chapter on Deuteronomy's attitude to the monarchy, where we challenged the view that it was conceived as an apologia for that institution, and with it the Jerusalem cult.

personal relationship with him in such a way as to be involved with him in the construction of their lives and destiny.

This basic assumption underlies the next point, namely, Deuteronomy's vision of an "order" in the universe that embraces all of life. This point may be summarily expressed as a correspondence between moral and religious uprightness (or "righteousness") and enjoyment of the good of creation (or "blessing"). The former is represented everywhere in Deuteronomy by the repeated calls to obey the commands of Yahweh, and the latter by the cameo pictures of plenty (e.g., 6:10–11; 8:7–10). This correspondence is well illustrated in 6:24–25.[13] Much of Deuteronomy is devoted to the development of this vision. It undergirds its laws, which are no mere code of regulations but enshrine profoundly the principles of love and self-denial—those themes that many commentators have seen as one of the hallmarks of the book.[14]

The reality of human freedom, however, implies that the harmonious vision may or may not be realized. Consequently, Deuteronomy not only holds out the prospect of weal, but also warns of woe. The place where these alternatives are most clearly set forth is in the "blessings and curses" of ch. 28, containing the full gamut of human experience from the conditions that make for contentment (vv. 1–15) to the greatest misery (vv. 16–68).

Deuteronomy is thus keenly aware of the dark side of human experience. Its depiction of human pain shows that the author is fully aware of the perplexity that characterizes other contemporary literature, both within and outside the

---

[13]See my *Law and Theology in Deuteronomy* (Sheffield: JSOT, 1984), 14–15. The idea is expounded at length by H. H. Schmid, *Gerechtigkeit als Weltordnung* (Tübingen: J. C. B. Mohr, 1968), especially p. 124.

[14]For the ethics of Deuteronomy, see M. Weinfeld, *Deuteronomy and the Deuteronomic School* (Oxford: Clarendon, 1972), 282–97; and for the theology of the laws, see McConville, *Law and Theology in Deuteronomy*, 78–87.

OT.[15] We shall see in a moment how much Deuteronomy wrestles with the apparent impossibility of hope, given human sinfulness. Its theism, however, ultimately resists the slide into mere perplexity. Rather, the various possible destinies are depicted in terms of Deuteronomy's understanding that God deals with human beings within history, both desiring their good and setting standards that allow them fateful choices. The adoption of the convention of the treaty-form serves this purpose. The author of a treaty can fulfill threats and promises as far as he is able; Yahweh, who controls all history, is the ultimate author of all weal and woe.

ELECTION AND COVENANT

A revelation of God in history cannot avoid particularity. It is no accident, therefore, that Deuteronomy takes as its primary datum God's election of Israel (1:8; 7:6), a historical beginning, and arcs forward from that point to the prospect of the same people's languishing in an exile that seems to be a historical finality (28:64–68). The form of the relationship that God adopts with his chosen people is that of covenant, giving expression to the need for mutual commitment in space and time. His choice of Israel is not motivated by any special qualification on their part (7:6–8; 9:4–6). Nevertheless, the promise God makes to them has its counterpart in command.[16] Indeed, his actions on Israel's behalf can hardly be conceptualized apart from the response that they are designed to elicit. Israel's occupation of the land is both a decree of God and an obligation laid upon the people (1:19–21), so much so that a failure to occupy the land is a failure of faith and obedience (1:26). The gift of the land is not a thing in itself, but initiates a scenario in which a people lives before

---

[15]E.g. Job; cf. also certain "wisdom" writings of the Ancient Near East.

[16]We argued in chapter 2 that it is impossible to drive a wedge between these two poles of a single reality.

their God in covenant faithfulness.[17] If, therefore, God's universe has an underlying order in which blessing and righteousness are proper complements, Israel is the arena in which he will make it manifest, and the covenant with them is the chosen means.

The story of Israel, of course, is one in which the people fail to live in covenant faithfulness. This is clear not only from the end of the story in 2 Kings, but at every point from the beginning to the end. The failure, of course, is not seen as the disappointment of the hopes of Deuteronomy, for Deuteronomy itself is not naively optimistic about the capacities of Israel to succeed. At the outset the book anticipates what we saw as a recurring feature of the story of Israel in DtH, namely, the people's inability to receive from God in faith and their corresponding tendency to trust their own perception of situations. Israel's reluctance to go and take the land when God commanded them to and when they would certainly have succeeded, gives way to an attempt to take it in their own strength when the moment has passed because there is no longer a sanction from God; the result is ignominious defeat (1:26–46; cf. Nu 13–14). This passage has a special significance in the book because of its prominent position, and it prepares for the concatenation of disasters related in DtH, which expose again and again the discrepancy between the possibilities of the way of faith and the dismal actualities of self-trust. Herein lies all the irony that we have found to be one of the pervading features of DtH—an irony born of an understanding of Israel as profoundly incapable of covenant faithfulness. Here, if anywhere, is a feature of the OT's understanding of history that distinguishes it from others in the ancient world, a self-consciousness not in the sense favored by Van Seters, who sees DtH as an apologia for the

---

[17]See McConville, *Law and Theology in Deuteronomy*, 12–13, especially on 18:14.

monarchy,[18] but in sharp contrast, one that is essentially critical.

Deuteronomy's perception of Israel's inability to be a faithful covenant partner is further the subject of chs. 9–10, a section that recalls the debacle of the apostasy at Sinai (Ex 32). In this connection, the author stresses that Israel has been singled out for the gift of the land, not because of her own virtue, but rather in spite of her lack of it, for they are a "stiffnecked" people (Dt 9:4–6). By placing this elaboration of Israel's failure at this point, before the long series of laws that they are required to keep, Deuteronomy seems deliberately to sharpen the dilemma that it sees, namely, how it can be that a people who cannot keep covenant should be given a land on the express condition that they do so. The alternatives placed before the people both at 11:26–32 and in ch. 28 seem to be mocked by a theology that claims Israel is constitutionally incapable of choosing the way of life. If ch. 28 were the end of the book, it would be a gloomy picture indeed.

GRACE IN THE END

But Deuteronomy 28 is not the end of the book, and in its continuation (especially in chs. 29–30) lies the answer to its perplexity about the condition and destiny of Israel. The first verse of this section (29:1) is crucial in the structure of the whole book, forming a bridge between the second and third addresses of Moses to Israel (4:44–28:68 and 29:1–30:20 respectively). This verse can be seen as both a retrospect on the second address and an introduction to the third. (Its double role is already suggested by a confusion in the OT versions as to whether it is the closing verse of ch. 28—28:69, as in MT—or the first verse in the next section—29:1, as in

---

[18]J. Van Seters, *In Search of History* (New Haven: Yale University Press, 1983), 289.

EVV). The "words of the covenant" are best explained as referring to Moses' preaching of the law given on Horeb, the substance of the long second address. Deuteronomy 29:1, therefore, is a kind of interpretation of the status of Moses' words as an authoritative interpretation of the decalogue (5:6–21, a passage placed, incidentally, at the beginning of the second address).

At the same time, however, this verse is clearly presupposed in what follows in ch. 29, especially because of the repetition several times of the word "covenant" (vv. 9, 12, 14, 21, 25).[19] In fact, it functions primarily to introduce a further exhortation to keep the covenant. Chapters 29–30, indeed, have many of the elements one expects to find in a covenantal text (i.e., historical prologue, 29:2–8; general stipulations, 29:9–15; specific stipulations, 29:16–19; the curse, 29:20–28; 30:1; the blessing, 30:1–10). What is the purpose, however, of this new exhortation?

The answer to this question is connected with what we observed a moment ago about the dilemma posed by a Deuteronomy that invites the covenant people to faithfulness, yet knows they cannot achieve it. Moses' third address puts a new angle on the call to obedience in at least two ways. First, it takes for granted that the people will indeed fail to be the true people of the covenant and that this will result in the full force of the curses of ch. 28 falling on them. Deuteronomy 30:1 makes this clear, for it thinks of the blessing and the curse no longer as alternative possibilities, but as successive realities in Israel's life.[20] That is, Israel will first know the blessing of God in their possession of the land, then the curse of God in its loss. Such a view of Israel's prospects is not surprising in view of 9:4–6.[21] It also affords an insight into

[19]See A. D. H. Mayes, *Deuteronomy*, NCB (London: Oliphants, 1979), 360–61.

[20]Ibid., 367–68. J. Wellhausen has also seen this; see his *Prolegomena to the History of Ancient Israel* (Edinburgh: A. and C. Black, 1885), 190–91.

[21]The idea of Israel's inevitable judgment because of her inability to keep the covenant is also present in the latter chapters of Deuteronomy (29:22–28; 32).

parts of DtH. David's reign, for example, has been interpreted as falling into two distinct periods: "David under the blessing," followed by "David under the curse."[22] Noth's understanding of the portrayal of Solomon was similar.[23] The very structure of Deuteronomy points to the beginning of the resolution of the tension created by the ending of ch. 28, a chapter that, in view of 9:4–6, suggested Israel's future was bleak.

Second, that tension is not resolved by the mere sequence of blessing and curse, but by what follows. Deuteronomy 30:2–3 pictures the people's repentance in exile, which in turn precipitates a restoration of their fortunes, here explicitly involving a return to the land. This structure immediately raises the question how that new restored situation might be any different from the old, the one that had had such wretched and apparently inevitable results. This, indeed, is the central problem posed by Deuteronomy, and we are therefore close to the heart of what may properly be called Deuteronomic theology. In addressing the problem, Deuteronomy shows that it espouses no crude or simplistic answers to difficult questions.

The crucial point in Deuteronomy's answer is in 30:6, the significance of which emerges by comparing it with 10:16. In both places the author uses the metaphor of the circumcision of the heart to convey the idea of true, inward devotion to the way of Yahweh. In 10:16 we read a simple exhortation to Israel: "Circumcise your hearts. . . ." In 30:6, however, a shift occurs, so that now Yahweh himself declares that *he* will take an initiative in this respect: "The LORD your God will circumcise your hearts and the hearts of your descendants," resulting in Israel's ability to obey the exhortation to love him

---

[22]R. A. Carlson, *David: The Chosen King* (Stockholm: Almqvist and Wikseel, 1964), 25.

[23]Noth, *The Deuteronomistic History* (Sheffield: JSOT, 1981), 58.

with all their heart and soul (an exhortation first made at
6:4–5).

The particular terms of 30:6 can hardly be accidental.
They propose an answer to the problem of Israel's infidelity
to the covenant that finds echoes elsewhere in the OT,
notably in Hosea (Hos 14:4) and especially in the new
covenant theology of Jeremiah (Jer 31:33; 32:39–40). These
places affirm that the answer to Israel's infidelity lies in God
himself. He will somehow enable his people ultimately to do
what they cannot do in their strength, namely, to obey him
out of the conviction and devotion of their own hearts.

Does this answer, then, run counter to the whole drift of
the book to this point, with its stress on the need for Israel to
hear and obey God's laws as free and responsible agents? On
the contrary, Deuteronomy will not abandon its commitment
to the vision of a people in free and harmonious relationship
with their God (30:8). This is clear from the development of
the argument in ch. 30. The first ten verses themselves, as the
immediate context of v. 6, contain conditions and exhortations (vv. 2, 10). It is no accident, however, that the passage
that speaks of Yahweh's initiative in enabling Israel to be
faithful is followed by one that contains the most explicit
statement in the whole book of *their ability* to obey his
commands (30:11–14); this, in turn, is followed by more
exhortations (vv. 15–20).

The relationship between 30:6 and 30:11–14 is not a
simple one. The former is part of Deuteronomy's glimpse into
the future (from the standpoint of those who are assembled on
the plains of Moab), its vision of a new hope for Israel on the
other side of the failures of its history from settlement to exile.
But vv. 11–14 come back to the Mosaic present, with the
typical urgent "today" (v. 11; the point is obscured by the
NIV translation), repeated in vv. 15–16. How does the vision
of a still future empowering of Israel by God affect the present
generation, one that with its successors has ahead of it a story
of moral and religious impotence?

The best answer to this question, I think, is not in terms of strict logical coherence, but of the structure of the book. The renewed exhortations in 30:11–14 must certainly be read in the light of both 9:4–6 (which 30:11–14 formally contradict) and of 30:1–10. Deuteronomy 30:11–14 state a truth in principle, but one that is negated in history by the character of Israel. The exhortation remains absolute, though we know that it can only ever have validity in a new arrangement that lies beyond both sin and judgment. When it finally gains this validity, it is a work of God's grace—"grace in the end."

Deuteronomy's ultimate solution to the problem posed by an errant covenant people gives a clue to reading DtH. This history, as we have seen, is the story that proves the contention of 9:4–6 and of ch. 32, a story with an inevitable outcome in disaster because of the overweening self-confidence of Israel. At the end of that story appears a portentous question: Does the fall of the ultimate covenantal curse of an exile mean that God has no further plans for the people he once chose? The books of 1, 2 Kings are not wholly pessimistic, because they contain the prayer of Solomon with its vision of a turning of the exiles' fortunes. However, this hope is muted in that no specific expectation of a return to the land is expressed; indeed, it seems to be carefully eschewed.[24] Other parts of DtH, we have argued, do not raise the question of exile directly, but deal with issues from other periods of the history, and therefore in this respect function to provide essential background in terms of causes. DtH, therefore, has no articulated hope regarding what, if anything, may lie beyond the ultimate covenantal sanction of the exile.[25] It is Deuteronomy itself that has the key to such a

[24]I have demonstrated this point in detail in my "1 Kings VIII 46-53 and the Deuteronomic Hope," *VT* 42 (1992), 67–79.

[25]This view is in contrast to those that find one or more exilic editions running through the books, according to the theories of Cross and Smend; see above, ch. 4.

hope, in its carefully re-expressed picture of covenantal conditions in chs. 29–30.

EXCURSUS: DEUTERONOMY AND THE CANAANITES

One of the great dilemmas confronting the modern reader of Deuteronomy is the apparent paradox in a book that on the one hand expounds in a profound way God's love for a people and his expectation of love in return, and on the other demands the destruction of those peoples who occupied the land that Israel was commanded to take. Is this a blind spot in the mind of the author, a failure by his own standards? And must the book at this point be pronounced unacceptable or primitive by a Christian reader?

A first step towards coming to an understanding of the passages in Deuteronomy (and indeed Joshua, Judges, and 1, 2 Samuel)[26] that command the slaughter of the Canaanites and other nations is to see them in the context of the theology of the book. The main categories that apply are the ideas of Yahweh as the only true God, of Yahweh as the God of history, and of his election of his people.

We have seen in our study of Joshua that Israel was by no means unique in the belief that their God fought their wars. We also saw an element of the hypothetical, ideal, or conventional in the language used of conquest.[27] One way to look at the OT's idea of Holy War is to see it as the Israelite counterpart to claims made for gods throughout the ancient world. This approach can apply to other aspects of OT religion. The regulations for sacrifice, for example, can be explained as the requirement that Israel bring her offerings not to any other god, but to Yahweh. In other words, the

---

[26]The idea of Holy War is obvious in Joshua, where Jericho and Ai are captured with great slaughter, and it is never far from the surface in Judges (e.g., Jdg 4; 16:30); cf. also 1Sa 15.

[27]See above, ch. 4.

formal and material side of worship was simply a given in the world of the OT; the only issue was whether worship was offered in the right manner, in terms both of the right God and of the right attitude. The OT's adoption of Holy War language may be partly explained in the same way, its point being that it is not any other god who has power to protect and deliver Israel, but only Yahweh. Since Israel was one nation among other nations, war was simply a given in international relations.

Two points follow from this in relation to the Holy War. First, it is part of Yahweh's polemic against other gods and vindicates his claim upon Israel; he is able to give what he has promised and is therefore worthy of the allegiance he requires. It is important to note in this connection that the command to destroy the Canaanites aims at the same time to destroy their religion. When Yahweh's *name* is to be honored at the place he will choose, the *names* of the gods of the land are to be blotted out from memory by the destruction of their rival places of worship (12:2–5). No quarter is to be given to the delusion that Baal is the one who has given the gifts that are really Yahweh's (cf. Hos 2:5, 8–9 [MT 7, 10–11]). Second, the Holy War is a reminder to Israel that they gain nothing in their own strength, but only as a gift from God.

Deuteronomy 7:2–3 itself hints that its Holy War theology has an element of the ideal or conventional about it, where a command to destroy the peoples of the land utterly is immediately followed by the somewhat less rigorous requirement that Israel make no "covenant" or marriages with them! This non-sequitur suggests that the first requirement might not be fully carried out. The point should not be over-pressed, however, for it would be far-fetched to argue that the command to destroy the peoples was not meant to have any historical reality whatever, but was only a metaphor. It is precisely Yahweh's power in war that is at stake. And it is possible that the mitigated commands in 7:2b–3 have an intended irony, foreseeing Israel's lack of rigor in implementing the "ban" (the devotion of the condemned peoples to Yahweh). On this view the point of 7:2–3 would be the opposite of mitigation and more in line with Samuel's severity in 1 Samuel 15.

To see the Holy War only as Israel's version of the divine wars of the ancient world, however, does not give sufficient account of it in terms of Deuteronomy. The Canaanites are to be destroyed not simply because they are in the way, but because they are condemned for their sin (9:4). The gift of Canaan to Israel is, by the same token, a specific judgment on the inhabitants of the land. The question is immediately raised, of course, why Israel is not also subject to the same judgment. Their own sinfulness is exposed in the very same passage in which the Canaanites are condemned for theirs. We have commented above on the paradox of the land being given precisely to a sinful people. The answer can only be in terms of Yahweh's plan ultimately to reveal his grace, something he will do in and through Israel, in history, and perhaps only possibly by such means as this. Israel in turn will fall victim to this very Holy War of Yahweh; that is the rationale behind the exile—the end of the Deuteronomic story (2 Kings 25).

A further point must be made, however, regarding the sinfulness of the Canaanites, namely, that a correspondence exists between the struggle of Yahwism with Canaanitism and the extirpation of Canaanite religion. This, the reader will recall, was one of the main themes of Deuteronomy. In a thoroughgoing way, Deuteronomy is conceived as an anti-Canaanite program. Canaanite religion is everywhere seen as a snare set to trap the Israelite nation and divert them from the path of Yahwism (7:4; 12:30; 13). The victory over Canaan, therefore, is not merely a demonstration of power, but also a vindication of the truth. Those very tenets of Yahwism that we saw distinguish it from Canaanite and other contemporary religions triumph in Yahweh's victory. History is indeed governed by the one and only God, who is not controlled by the institutions of his own religion, but who freely disposes over all history and creation and who invites a people into a true, bilateral relationship.

The confrontation of Yahweh with the Canaanites and their gods belongs in a subtle way to the affirmation of his rule in history. All religions of the ancient Near East picture a primeval conflict between the creator-god and the forces of chaos.[28] The OT's narratives of Creation and Flood correspond to these epics of creation and chaos, but differ according to the distinctive emphases of OT religion that we have tried to express above, especially in that they see all reality under the sway of the one omnipotent God. One dimension of this distinctive character of OT religion is its tendency to historicize the primeval or fundamental conflicts. Thus, the OT Flood narrative places the threat of the earth's submersion in the waters of creation in a story that is firmly rooted in the past and that finishes with a promise that no such thing will happen again (Ge 9:15). This is in contrast to the other polytheistic religions with their tendency to confuse elements of the created order with personal agencies (the Sea, or great Deep, is depicted both as the natural element and as a personality, which, by definition, has some independence of the deity that confronts it and therefore continues to threaten).[29]

The conflict with the Canaanites has analogies, I think, with the biblical Flood narrative, in the sense that it enshrines Yahweh's encounter with Baal in a historical conflict with Canaanites and all things Canaanite. The issue is a confrontation between the forces of truth, salvation, and blessing,

---

[28]In the Mesopotamian creation epic, *Enûma elish*, Marduk slays the chaos-monster Tiamat and creates the world from her carcass (see *ANET*, 60–72); in Canaan, Baal engages in mortal combat with the sea-monster Yam (*ANET*, 129–31); cf. J. C. L. Gibson, *Canaanite Myths and Legends*, 2d ed. (Edinburgh: T. and T. Clark, 1978).

[29]B. S. Childs, *Myth and Reality in the Old Testament* (London: SCM, 1960), 33, 36, cf. 37–42.

and those of falsehood, destruction, and curse, and in characteristic biblical fashion it is played out in history. The destruction of the Canaanites, therefore, is not a vindictive genocide. God is not depicted here as destroying Canaanites just because they are not Israelites. In fact, Deuteronomy contains legislation that enables certain foreigners to become members of the worshiping covenant community (23:7, though see also vv. 3–6) and enjoins compassion on all "aliens" (14:29; 24:20).

When we have tried to understand the destruction of the Canaanites from within Deuteronomy's world of concerns, it remains to consider how it relates to wider themes in OT theology. One of the great tensions within the OT is the one between the need to maintain the purity of Israel and the mission of Israel to bring the worship of Yahweh to other nations. The latter theme occurs in different ways in several places. The promise to Abraham (incidentally, an important part of Deuteronomy's conceptual furniture) both singles out his descendants for blessing and a special role in history and pronounces that through them "all peoples on earth will be blessed" (Gen 12:3). This "universalistic" theme in OT theology (in the sense of a divine plan of salvation that embraces other nations as well as Israel) is developed particularly in the book of Isaiah (2:2–4; 40–55),[30] and it is also present in Jonah.

Deuteronomy, however, is one of those parts of the OT (along with, most obviously, Ezra and Nehemiah) that guard first and foremost the purity of true religion. If Deuteronomy is strong on this topic of religion, perhaps it may be conceded that in some sense it is deficient on the other side of the tension, for it does not in itself reveal the love of God for all humanity.[31] It does not seem to me to be necessary, however,

---

[30]For a discussion of Israel's "mission" to the nations in Isaiah see A. Gelston, "The Missionary Message of Second Isaiah," *SJT* 18 (1965), 308–18.

[31]See John Goldingay, *Theological Diversity and the Authority of the Old Testament* (Grand Rapids: Eerdmans, 1987), 134–66, for an "evaluative" approach to Deuteronomy, where he takes up this precise issue.

to postulate a conflict of opinion as between different parties within Judaism on this issue, at least in the OT period. Rather, on a broad canvas of OT theology, one may think of an "economy" within which God aims ultimately to save the world, but chooses to do so by means of the election of a people through whom he is known and his worship cultivated.[32] The slaughter of the Canaanites cannot but be repugnant to the modern reader. But perhaps, when put in the perspective just outlined, it can be seen as the dark, other side of God's love, a love that is solemn, even fierce, but whose end is the salvation of the world.

---

[32]I have developed this idea in my "The Shadow of the Curse: A Key to Old Testament Theology," *Evangel* 3/1 (1985), 2–5.

◆ 6 ◆

Deuteronomic Theology and the New Testament

As is well known, Deuteronomy is cited in the NT more frequently than any other OT book. Its influence, however, cannot be measured only in terms of direct quotations. Indeed, the relationship between Deuteronomy and the NT is as complicated as the wider question of the relationship between the OT and the NT. Studies of how the two testaments are related show that their interconnection cannot be stated in any simple or single formula.[1] Deuteronomy makes its presence felt in the NT in a number of ways, at the level of its fundamental concerns and of individual verses cited by the NT writers.

UNDERLYING THEMES

At the level of Deuteronomy's main themes, the connections are sometimes so basic that it might seem farfetched to describe them as linked directly with Deuteronomy. For

---

[1]See John E. Goldingay, *Approaches to Old Testament Interpretation*, 2d ed. (Leicester: Apollos, 1990), for his fivefold approach to interpreting the OT: the OT as faith, way of life, story of salvation, Scripture, and witness to Christ.

example, the NT's very monotheism, scarcely to be taken for granted even in its own world, needs no special justification in the NT precisely because it can rest on the legacy of the OT, to which Deuteronomy made no small contribution (Deut 6:4). The NT writers sometimes speak directly about idolatry, and when they do, Deuteronomy can sometimes be detected underlying those statements. When Paul deplores pagan sacrifices to "demons" (1Co 10:20), he may have in mind an allusion to the Song of Moses (Dt 32:17). Or again, when he warns the Corinthian Christians not to be "yoked together with unbelievers" (2Co 6:14), he probably has in mind the Deuteronomic prohibition of yoking together different kinds of animals in agriculture (Dt 22:10). While this is a somewhat non-literal application of that ancient provision, Paul nevertheless catches an important strain of Deuteronomic thought, its horror of syncretism.

Similarly, in its assumption that God acts decisively in history, the NT stands on the shoulders of the OT's development of a theology of God's action in history by which, as we have seen, it can be distinguished from the ideologies of Israel's neighbors. The "Christ-event" may thus be seen as one of those saving acts of God (such as the Exodus from Egypt) that were the stuff of the OT story, even if it surpasses all of them in its scope and significance.[2] To take another example, even the NT's belief that human beings may know God, enter into a relationship with him, and in that context have a destiny that promises to satisfy their profoundest longings, builds upon the gains of the OT writers, in which again Deuteronomy has played an important part.

---

[2]This is the approach of von Rad, in his *Old Testament Theology* (London and Edinburgh: Oliver and Boyd, 1962, 1965), 2.319–30.

ETHICS

There are, however, also specific ways in which Deuteronomy becomes visible in the NT. One straightforward way is in terms of ethics. The manner in which this happens is complex, being partly by contrast and partly by assimilation. An example of contrast is Jesus' citation of the divorce law of Deuteronomy 24:1–4 (Mt 19:7–9; cf. 5:31–2), in which he appears to set a higher standard than the OT law. His treatment of the divorce law resembles the "But I tell you" sayings of the Sermon on the Mount (Mt 5:21–48). Deuteronomy, for example, has its version of the so-called *lex talionis* (Dt 19:21), the law that is famously superseded by Jesus' command to turn the other cheek to an aggressor and even to lend him assistance (Mt 5:38–42). In a similar way, a prohibition of oath-breaking (Dt 23:21) becomes a prohibition of oath-making (Mt 5:33–37).

However, the relationship between Deuteronomy's laws and the NT commands is not expressed entirely in terms of contrast. We are alerted to this by the introduction to the above-mentioned section of the Sermon on the Mount, where Jesus says that he has come to "fulfill" the Law and the Prophets, not to abolish them (Mt 5:17). And it is likely that Jesus saw his preaching of the law of God in general as bringing out its full force rather than diminishing it. His words on murder and adultery (Mt 5:21–30) are cases in point.

Deuteronomy may thus be seen as contributing positively to Jesus' moral teaching and to the ethics of the NT. One fundamental principle of Deuteronomic ethics becomes a prominent NT principle: the idea of self-denial on behalf of others, which in turn brings the blessing of God upon oneself. This theme is well illustrated by the law of the release of slaves (Dt 15:12–18), in which God commands the master of slaves not only to release them after a period of six years, but also to provide liberally for them out of his own substance in order that they may be able to become economically viable once again. With the command comes an assurance: "And the LORD your God will bless you in everything you do" (v. 18). The thinking in this particular law, furthermore, well represents the spirit of the laws in Deuteronomy.[3] A similar thought, however, also underlies 2 Corinthians 9:9–15. The context is not one of slavery, but it concerns generosity to those who are in need and, like Deuteronomy, gives reassurance that through God's grace there is no loss in sincere giving (vv. 8–11).

The subject of slavery deserves consideration in its own right. The law in Deuteronomy 15 just cited is interesting not only for its command to give generously, but also because of its intention that there should be *no* slavery in Israel. Deuteronomy insists that all Israelites form a brotherhood (Dt 1:16; 3:18, 20; 10:9). This implies a right on the part of every Israelite to share in the blessings of the covenant community, e.g., the freedom to enjoy the good things of the land in peace. The most concentrated appeal to the idea of brotherhood is in the immediate context of the law regarding slave-release (15:3, 7, 9, 11—concerning the release of debts) and is carried over into that law itself (v. 12). Indeed, the idea of Israelite brotherhood, introduced at the beginning of the law regarding slaves, stands over the provision that follows, as if to say that slavery in itself (i.e., the "ownership" of one human being by another) is in irreconcilable tension with that basic constitutional point. Deuteronomy's theology of brotherhood can hardly be accused of condoning slavery. On the contrary, it is revolutionary. And yet, because misfortune could reduce anyone in a subsistence culture to life-threatening penury, systems were needed to rescue the victims. Deuteronomy's permission of a controlled institution

---

[3]See McConville, *Law and Theology in Deuteronomy* (Sheffield: JSOT, 1984), 15–18.

of slavery is, in fact, a pragmatic measure, belonging in the context of its humanitarian package.

Paul's approach to the problem of the runaway slave Onesimus in his letter to Philemon, the master of Onesimus, has much in common with the Deuteronomic provision. Paul's insistence that Onesimus return to Philemon may seem like a compromise with a tyrannical institution. Yet here too the concept of brotherhood renders true slavery an impossibility, and Philemon is exhorted to take Onesimus back, "no longer as a slave, but better than a slave, as a dear brother . . . a brother in the Lord" (v. 16). Once again, it may be argued, Deuteronomy has fed the thinking of this NT writer.

The law of the release of slaves suggests a different line of inquiry regarding the Deuteronomic attitude to wealth (though by no means limited to the law in question). We have seen how much the Deuteronomic hope was expressed in terms of land and of this-worldly well-being. How does this theme relate to a NT ethic that so often plays down this-worldly wealth on the grounds that true wealth is stored up in heaven (e.g., Mt 6:19–21)? In particular, does Deuteronomy encourage the unhealthy thought that God gives material riches to those whom he especially favors—and conversely, that those who are not rich are not so favored?

In an issue as complex as this one, we may make two brief points. First, the contrast between the OT as "worldly" and the NT as "spiritual" is a false one. The OT's theology of creation, according to which God made a "good" earth and put human beings in it to enjoy it (Ge 1), is never quite lost in the NT. This emerges not only from the Apocalyptic vision of "a new heaven and a new earth" (Rev 21:1), so clearly taking up the language of Genesis 1:1, but also from parts of the teaching and life of Jesus. It is often pointed out that, in the well-known beatitude, what the meek inherit can be translated as "the land" (Mt 5:5). The hope placed before the first disciples, therefore, was indeed fuller and richer than the OT

saints had known and served to console them in circumstances in which they had little prospect of material well-
being; yet it was not necessarily wholly discontinuous with it.

Second, Deuteronomy is seriously misunderstood if it is
seen merely as a kind of sanction for the making and enjoying
of wealth. As we have seen, Deuteronomy knows all too well
the moral dangers of plenty. The problem with what is
sometimes called "prosperity theology," i.e., the belief that
God always materially rewards the righteous and that such
rewards can be held out as the sure consequence of acts of
obedience to God, is that Deuteronomy clearly indicates that
such rewards may not be counted on. As soon as such
calculation enters the relationship between God and the
faithful, it is a sure sign that the true requirement of
Deuteronomy has been missed, namely, a devotion of the
heart to God and a disposition to do good to one's neighbor.
If, therefore, Deuteronomy is characterized as "materialis-
tic," it has been misrepresented. This book is not, after all, far
from Jesus' own command to "seek first [God's] kingdom and
his righteousness, and all these things will be given to you as
well" (Mt 6:33).

KINGDOM, ELECTION, AND COVENANT

One of the ways in which the OT relates to the NT is in
their shared story—the story of redemption that is played out
in history. Jesus saw himself as fulfilling promises expressed
in the OT, as the story of the Emmaus road encounter makes
clear (Lk 24:27), even if the manner of his fulfillment of them
demands careful consideration.[4] One direct promise of Deuteronomy, that God would raise up a prophet like Moses after
him (Dt 18:15, 18), was applied to Jesus by Peter (Ac 3:22–3)

---

[4]The way in which Jesus fulfills OT prophecy is not straightforward. For
a helpful orientation to the question, see Goldingay, *Approaches to Old
Testament Interpretation*, 115–22.

and implicitly by John the Baptist in his denial that he himself had come in that role (Jn 1:21).

The idea of Jesus as the fulfillment of expectations engendered by the OT is by no means exhausted by specific links of this sort. More generally, it has to be traced at the level of themes. In the case of Deuteronomy, some of its great themes, when traced into the NT, have a new Christological orientation. The Deuteronomic connection between hearing the word and receiving life, for example (Dt 30:20), recurs as hearing *Christ's* word and receiving *eternal* life (Jn 5:24–25). Deuteronomy may not have known that God's gift of life was not limited even by the grave. (Here, perhaps, is another "deficiency," comparable with its lack of a "mission-theology."[5]) Yet Deuteronomy knew "life" as God's purpose for his people, knew life qualitatively, and knew the inseparable connection between it and righteousness.

Our consideration of the NT's fulfillment of a story leads us back to Deuteronomy's view of history. God was the Great King (Dt 33:5),[6] who had entered into a relationship with a people on the basis of election and in the shape of a covenant. The great Deuteronomic themes of kingdom, election, and covenant continue into the NT, where they are interpreted Christologically. The conferral of a "kingdom" on the disciples (Lk 22:29–30) suggests that they are seen as "Israel," or the nucleus of an eschatological Israel, who share in the kingship of Christ. The idea also of God's election of the weak and undeserving (Dt 7:6–8) is used by Paul of the church when he says: "God chose the foolish things of the world to shame the wise; God chose the weak things of the world to shame the strong. He chose the lowly things of this world and the despised things—and the things that are not—

---

[5]See above, ch. 5.

[6]His kingship is also implied by the approximation of Deuteronomy to the form of a vassal-treaty; see ch. 2, above.

to nullify the things that are" (1Co 1:27–8). This election, furthermore, is "in Christ Jesus" (v. 30).[7]

The way in which the Deuteronomic idea of covenant occurs in the NT requires special consideration. One of the obvious ways in which the theme of covenant appears is in terms of the new covenant. Both Paul and the writer of Hebrews relate the significance of Jesus' life and atonement to Jeremiah's preaching of a new covenant (1Co 11:25; 2Co 3:6; Heb 8:8; 9:15; 12:24; cf. Jer 31:31–34). The tendency of the NT arguments in this regard is strongly contrastive. The "old covenant" (2Co 3:14) is associated with the "letter" that kills, as opposed to the Spirit who gives life (3:6). In Hebrews the Mosaic covenant is systematically shown to be inferior to that which is brought into existence by Jesus. As the true High Priest who serves in the true tabernacle, heaven, Jesus demonstrates that the covenant centered on the tabernacle and temple of Israel is but a passing shadow (Heb 8).

However, on closer inspection the NT bears marks of continuity with the OT idea as we have tried to expound it, especially in Deuteronomy. At the outset, it is important to observe that the covenantal idea may be present even where it is not obvious from the specific terms used. That is, the NT's theology of covenant is not exhausted by its use of the new covenant idea. The point is clearest in Paul's letter to the Romans.

Recent treatments of Romans have shown that the letter has much to do with the understanding of covenant.[8] It concerns the identity of the covenant people and the basis on which their relationship with God may be said to be characterized by "righteousness" (*dikaiosynē*). The basic ideas

---

[7]Notice a further link between the 1 Corinthians passage and the one in Deuteronomy in the idea of holiness brought into connection with election (1Co 1:30; Dt 7:6).

[8]N. T. Wright, "The Messiah and the People of God" (Ph.D. dissertation, Oxford University, 1980); J. D. G. Dunn, *Romans 1–8*, WBC (Dallas: Word Books, 1988), lxiv–lxxii.

in the argument are already familiar from the pages of the OT. We have seen that the covenantal relationship between Israel and Yahweh was to be marked by "righteousness" (Dt 6:24–25; Heb. *ts˒dāqâ*).[9] That passage illustrated the close connection between a right relationship with Yahweh and the enjoyment of the covenant blessings, and maintaining that relationship had much to do with keeping Yahweh's commands. Who, then, forms the covenant people of God? Is it, by definition, the Jews, and are they "righteous" through their observance of the Law as they understand it? Paul argues rather that the covenant people are those who are made "righteous" by faith in Jesus Christ.

Does Romans, therefore, reject the Deuteronomic picture of covenant? Obviously, in one sense Romans appears to be like Hebrews, for it contrasts the revelation of salvation in Christ with that which was revealed by the Law of the OT (Ro 3:21). In the course of Paul's argument, the capacity of the Law to save is seriously questioned (2:17–27). Justification (or "righteousness") comes not by observing the Law, but by faith (3:20, 27).

Paul's use of the OT, however, is complex, for in some measure his argument depends on a continuity of ideas between the OT and NT. Justification itself (the declaration of being "righteous" before God) is a case in point. The righteousness of God, formerly revealed in the Law as that right relationship between God and Israel, is now revealed in Christ. The righteousness of God has not changed, only the manner of its revelation. Properly understood, it never was a thing to be won by human effort, but it was a divine, saving gift (Ps 143:1); that Paul agrees with this may be further inferred from Romans 3:31. In setting forth the Gospel, therefore, Paul is not only saying that something decisively new has happened in Christ, but also that the Jews with whom he is conducting his hypothetical debate are misunder-

---

[9]See above, ch. 5, n. 13.

standing their own Scriptures. Paul insists that a true "Jew is one inwardly; and circumcision is circumcision of the heart" (2:29). Both Deuteronomy and Jeremiah had seen this clearly (Dt 10:16; 30:6; Jer 4:4).

The question may still be asked whether Paul's understanding of righteousness and the covenant is truly in keeping with that of Deuteronomy. We may pursue this question by considering Romans 10:5–10, the tip of the iceberg of Paul's understanding of Deuteronomy. On the face of it, Paul opposes one OT passage to another. The quotation in 10:5b ("The man who does these things will live by them") is taken from Leviticus 18:5, but the thought is also close to Deuteronomy 4:1 and 6:24. Against this, Paul then alludes to Deuteronomy 30:12–14. This latter passage, as we have seen, proclaims the possibility of Israel keeping the commandments.[10] Paul understands it in relation to Christ. The "word" is related, not to the commandments given by Moses, but to the gospel, "the word of faith we are proclaiming" (v. 8). Paul focuses on the terms "word" and "heart" in the Deuteronomy passage in order to pursue his main point that righteousness—a true relationship with God—comes not by the effort of keeping the Law, but by faith.

Has Paul, therefore, set one part of Deuteronomy against another, or indeed significantly altered the plain sense of Deuteronomy 30:11–14? He has, it seems, deliberately minimized the language about keeping the commandments by omitting v. 11 and the phrase "so that you may obey it" at the end of v. 14.[11] As Dunn insists, Deuteronomy 30:11–14 *is* about keeping the commandments, and in this respect is not different from Leviticus 18:5 or Deuteronomy 4:1, with which, for the sake of his argument, Paul contrasts it.[12] However, Dunn argues that the antithesis between law and

---

[10]See above, ch. 5.

[11]Dunn, *Romans 9–16*, WBC (Dallas: Word Books, 1988), 613.

[12]Ibid.

faith in Romans is not so great as it first appears: "He can describe [Israel's] relationship with God not unfairly or wholly negatively in terms of 'righteousness from the law.' "[13] The law is not nullified by faith but fulfilled by it. Paul objects not to the commandment as such, but only if it is understood as works. His use of Deuteronomy 30:12–14 is suitable to his purpose because it lends itself to an understanding of righteousness as a gift of God and of the requirement to keep the law as met by faith. That he does not regard these verses as somehow exceptional within Deuteronomy is confirmed by his use of the words "Do not say in your heart" (Dt 9:4; cf. 8:17, RSV) to introduce the quotation from 30:12–14, thus drawing on other passages that know that a true response to God is an affair of the heart.

Paul, therefore, is not hostile to the Law as such, but only to a false understanding of it. It would be misguided to think that he regarded the Deuteronomic exposition of the place of the Law as false. On the contrary, we have seen that Deuteronomy is far from thinking that righteousness (i.e., a true relationship with God) is achieved by works of the law. Its understanding of the weakness of Israel with respect to the keeping of the covenant is fully in line with Paul's view that all need a salvation from God that is apart from observing the Law.

We can go further, for in our interpretation of the Deuteronomy passage we saw that that book was itself reflecting on rather similar issues to those that interested Paul. Deuteronomy knows well that the only acceptable response to God is a response from the heart (Dt 6:5; 10:16). However, it poses the problem of a covenantal relationship in which Israel is unable in their own strength to make such a response. Deuteronomy 30:11–14, as we saw, was part of its answer to that problem, following as it did upon 30:1–10, which had dealt with Israel's inability to keep the law in

---

[13]Ibid., 612.

terms somewhat similar to the new covenant theology of Jeremiah.[14] The writer of these verses thus put the demand for law-keeping in a new context, one that recognized that the "nearness" of the commandment was attributable to the gift of God. Deuteronomy 30:11–14 affirms Israel's capacity to respond adequately to God's command, because it knows that in the end God will "circumcise [their] hearts" (30:6).

The appropriateness of Paul's use of the passage thus emerges the more strongly. Paul also knows that an adequate response to God, a response of faith, is possible, made so by the revelation of God's righteousness in Christ. Yet, in that Deuteronomy 30:11–14 reiterates the command to keep covenant, it also "upholds the law" (cf. Ro 3:31). In sum, neither "Moses" nor Paul diminishes the need for the covenant relationship to be fully realized. Moses knew that some new act of God was needed in order to achieve the goal; Paul knows that that act is the coming of the gospel of Christ, with its promise of life from the dead, brought to fruition in a people that knew no racial or traditional boundaries.

CONCLUSIONS

We have seen a number of ways in which the NT adopts or presupposes ideas well known to Deuteronomy. This was true first at the level of fundamental theological themes, such as the belief that God is knowable and has a purpose in history. Second, it was true in relation to ethical principles; a careful reading of Deuteronomy could contribute to an understanding of, for example, the relationship between piety and wealth. (Here is an instance, incidentally, of the Law continuing to have validity in the Christian life).[15] Third, there were specific theological connections, where topics in

---

[14]See above, ch. 5.

[15]For more on this, see Goldingay, *Approaches to Old Testament Interpretation*, 38–65.

Deuteronomy's theology were interpreted Christologically. Such an interpretation of Deuteronomy, however, was not an abolition of its thought, but rather a fulfillment of it.

Finally, it has not been my purpose to suggest that the OT in general, or Deuteronomy in particular, has not been surpassed by the NT. My point has been that the relationship between the testaments, and indeed the intentions of the NT writers, are misunderstood when they are stated only in terms of contrast. It is clear that Romans is revolutionary compared with Deuteronomy in its understanding that God's salvation comes to the Gentiles, and also in the sense in which salvation was understood; Deuteronomy was resolutely inward-looking by comparison, to put the matter mildly. We have had cause, for example, to consider its attitude to the Canaanite peoples as a special problem.[16] Nevertheless, we have found that in its thinking about the relationship between God and the people of his choice it bears strong similarities to parts of the NT and may even shed light upon those parts.

---

[16]See above, ch. 5.

◆ 7 ◆
Conclusions

Our profile of Deuteronomic theology was hard won. It could not simply be equated with the "theology of Deuteronomy" nor confined to a study of that book. Rather, it posed a basic question about the development of religious thought in ancient Israel. Was Deuteronomy the presiding genius of Israelite religion from an early period, the last testament of Mosaic covenantal thought that informed and flowed into the profoundest work of the prophets? Or was it the product of tidy-minded scholars, a desperate last stand of legalism in the century of foreboding before the fall of Judah?

Our study put a serious question mark against the association of the book with the events of the seventh century B.C. in general and the reform of Josiah in particular. The appearance of scholarly unanimity on the surface dissolved on closer inspection, when precise occasions and settings were sought. This, we argued, was because Deuteronomy does not in fact furnish the desired evidence for a seventh century date.

This part of the investigation showed, furthermore, how much a view of the setting of Deuteronomy affected the understanding of its essential theological orientation. It has been variously seen as a book of promise or of legalistic requirement, as a pro-establishment tract or a subversive critique of the establishment. In such arguments, it could even be on both sides at the same time because of the successive contributions of different groups to its final form.

A satisfying estimate of the theology of Deuteronomy, therefore, required a position to be taken on its origin and composition. We found no good objections to the view that Deuteronomy was known at an early stage of Israel's history, and we noted adequate reasons to think that its ideas were exerting an influence on issues in Israel from the time of the judges on. Deuteronomic theology, therefore, could be described, first, in terms of the interplay of ideas within the book itself, where promise was held in tension with command, and the exercise of temporal power was both mandated and laid under constraint. The book was a program for Israel's life in its land, based on an understanding of history in terms of covenant with God, who alone was powerful and who desired to bless his people. It both affirmed God's sovereignty in Israel's affairs and was a charter for their lifestyle.

Second, Deuteronomic theology could be understood in terms of its application to various periods and issues in Israel's life. Studied thus, in the books known as the Deuteronomistic History (Joshua to 2 Kings), it proved to be seminal rather than rigid, and those books themselves could be individual in their theological thinking when compared with Deuteronomy. The two books of Kings, for example, had their own, somewhat muted, expression of hope for the future, reflecting, no doubt, their exilic situation. Deuteronomic theology could therefore be seen as a kind of dialogue within a tradition. This understanding of a Deuteronomic dialogue, however, is distinct from that which sees the book itself, and the other books of DtH, as composite works, juxtaposing contradictory views.

It is not necessary, in these concluding observations, to repeat the profile of Deuteronomic theology offered in ch. 5, but only to draw out some implications of it. Deuteronomy laid the foundation for much of biblical theology with its powerful network of concepts: its view of God, knowable through his own revelation of himself and giving salvation and blessing to a people in dynamic relationship with himself, in the context of a purpose that embraces all of history from election and the promise to consummation. Here is a "salvation-history" that provides natural contact points for Christology. For the Christian Church, God's "chosen people" today (1Pe 2:9), the covenant with the one true God is a new covenant in Christ, himself the incarnate God, the Word made flesh, who in his resurrection has revealed the meaning and end of history.

History, then, has no meaning apart from this powerful, personal, and gracious God. This picture calls forth worship and trust. Yet this "salvation-history" is neither determinism nor a recipe for quietistic admiration. It is call as well as promise. Both Deuteronomy and the NT preserve this balance carefully. On the one hand, God's will will be done; on the other, human choices remain real and consequential. If it were otherwise, there could be no human dignity. These two sides of biblical theology form, certainly, an unfathomable paradox. But it is just this paradox that Deuteronomy explores in its unique fashion and that is missed when the book is gratuitously broken up into competing, irreconcilable theological strands.

Our view of Deuteronomy has consequences at various levels. First, it affects the way in which we understand events and human activity in the world. A biblical view of history presents a challenge to other prevailing views, as much today as when Deuteronomy opposed Canaanite idolatry. The powerful ideas that have captured minds in the present century hardly need to be rehearsed. If the retreat of Marxism in Europe has left a vacuum, there are brands of nationalism, materialism, and even religious affiliations that are ready to rush in and take its place. Often, these powerful systems of ideas are more than practical aspirations, embodying claims to interpret the meaning of human life in the world. Sometimes they imply systems of human organization (whether political, religious, or economic) whose status is above question. In this sense they make absolute counterclaims to those that God makes upon his world, even borrowing the language of freedom, promise, salvation, and destiny. Such anthropocentric "theologies" of salvation are the counterfeit "names" that fall under biblical condemnation, so that the "Name" of the true author of human destiny might be enthroned (Dt 12:3, 5).

In the foregoing I have claimed that no human institution or system can be regarded as sacrosanct. This, I believe, is the inevitable application of Deuteronomy's provisions for both the central sanctuary of Israel and for the leadership of the king. Regarding the first, the name of Jerusalem is not so much as mentioned in the book. Jerusalem has no *necessary* claim in the OT (any more than in the modern world) to be the place where God dwells. It became so only by his sovereign choice, and by the same prerogative can cease to be so. The prophets, in preaching this very point (see Jer 7:1–15), are merely drawing out the implications of Deuteronomy. Nor has the king an unchallengeable status. He too rules by God's choice (Dt 17:15), and then only insofar as he accepts the ultimate authority of God and is open to his Word.

However, it would be wrong to infer from these points that all human authority and organization of society is, in itself, under condemnation. On the contrary, Deuteronomy calls human beings to organize themselves according to the Word of God. It contains, albeit in archaic dress, a mandate for political, economic, social, and religious life. This is the implication of its legislation about administration of the law (1:9–18; 17:8–13), equitable distribution of goods (14:28–29), brotherhood in the covenant (15:1–18), and religious celebration that acknowledges God as the author of all good (16:1–17).

The paradox, therefore, in Deuteronomy's insistence on God's sovereign "choice" as decisive in history and its equal insistence on the reality of human responsibility takes flesh in contemporary living. Christians believe that history is moving infallibly towards an "end" (both *eschaton* and *telos*). Yet we must be involved inextricably in the countless decisions, even compromises, that form the texture of that history.

I said in the opening chapter that the present volume was written in the immediate aftermath of the revolutionary events in Eastern Europe that brought first the Berlin wall, then the very center of Communist power, crashing to ruins. Associated events (especially the war in Yugoslavia) have taught us never to indulge in unthinking euphoria about these things. Nevertheless, they are at the very least a parable illustrating the impermanence of human structures that seemed for a time inviolable. More than that, they are, to the eye of faith, a pointer to the rule in history of a God who will not tolerate for long the pretensions of any system that openly defies his claims upon the hearts and lives of his creatures. In pulling down the bastions of self-serving human power, God leaves one more witness to himself. He is the same God who will establish his kingdom on earth finally in Christ. Knowing him, we not only engage fully with every aspect of human life, but we also believe him regarding the ultimate meaning of it all. There is indeed grace in history in the end.

◆ Bibliography ◆

Ackroyd, P. R. *Exile and Restoration*. London: SCM, 1968.

Albrektson, B. *History and the Gods*. Lund: Gleerup, 1967.

Alt, A. "Die Heimat des Deuteronomiums." Pp. 250–75 in Vol. 2 of his *Kleine Schriften zur Geschichte des Volkes Israel*. Munich: C. H. Beck'sche Verlagsbuchhandlung, 1953.

Andersen, F. I., and D. N. Freedman. *Hosea*. AB. New York: Doubleday, 1980.

Anderson, A. A. *2 Samuel*. WBC. Dallas: Word Books, 1989.

Anderson, B. W., and W. Harrelson eds. *Israel's Prophetic Heritage* (Festschrift for J. Muilenburg). New York: Harper Bros., 1962.

Anderson, G. W. *A Critical Introduction to the Old Testament*. London: Duckworth, 1959.

Bächli, O. *Israel und die Völker*. Zurich: Zwingli Verlag, 1962.

————. *Amphiktyonie im alten Testament*. Basel: Friedrich Reinhardt Verlag, 1977.

Baltzer, K. *The Covenant Formulary*. Oxford: Blackwell, 1971.

Bertholet, A. *Deuteronomium*. KHAT. Freiburg: Mohr, 1899.

Bimson, J. J. "The Origins of Israel in Canaan: An Examination of Recent Theories." *Themelios* 15 (1989), 4–15.

Blenkinsopp, J. *A History of Prophecy in Israel*. London: SPCK, 1984.

Braulik, G. "Die Abfolge der Gesetze in Deuteronomium 12–26 und der Dekalog." Pp. 252–72 in N. Lohfink, ed., *Das Deuteronomium*.

————. *Die Mittel Deuteronomischer Rhetorik*. Rome: Biblical Institute Press, 1978.

Bright, J. "The Date of the Prose Sermons of Jeremiah." *JBL* 70 (1951), 15–35.

Bronner, L. *The Stories of Elijah and Elisha*. Leiden: Brill, 1968.

Brueggemann, W. *The Land.* Philadelphia: Fortress, 1977.

————. "2 Samuel 21–24; An Appendix of Deconstruction?" *CBQ* 50 (1988), 383–97.

Buber, M. *The Kingship of God.* London: Allen and Unwin, 1967.

Butler, T. C. *Joshua.* WBC. Waco: Word Books, 1983.

Carlson, R. A. *David: The Chosen King.* Stockholm: Almquist and Wikseel, 1964.

Childs, B. S. *Introduction to the Old Testament as Scripture.* London: SCM, 1979.

————. *Myth and Reality in the Old Testament.* London: SCM, 1960.

Cholewinski, A. *Heiligkeitsgesetz und Deuteronomium.* Rome: Biblical Institute Press, 1976.

Clements, R. E. *Deuteronomy.* Old Testament Guides. Sheffield: JSOT, 1989.

————. "Deuteronomy and the Jerusalem Cult Tradition." *VT* 15 (1965), 300–12.

————. *God and Temple.* Oxford: Blackwell, 1965.

Craigie, P. C. *The Book of Deuteronomy.* NICOT. Grand Rapids: Eerdmans, 1976.

Cross, F. M. *Canaanite Myth and Hebrew Epic.* Cambridge, Mass.: Harvard University Press, 1973.

Crüsemann, F. *Der Widerstand gegen das Königtum.* Neukirchen: Neukirchener Verlag, 1978.

DeVries, S. J. *1 Kings.* WBC. Waco: Word Books, 1985.

Dietrich, W. *Prophetie und Geschichte.* Göttingen: Vandenhoeck and Ruprecht, 1972.

Driver, S. R. *A Critical and Exegetical Commentary on Deuteronomy.* ICC. Edinburgh: T. and T. Clark, 1895.

Dumbrell, W. J. *Covenant and Creation.* Exeter: Paternoster, 1984.

————. " 'In those days there was no king in Israel; every man did what was right in his own eyes.' The Purpose of the Book of Judges Reconsidered." *JSOT* 25 (1983), 23–33.

Dumermuth, F. "Zur deuteronomischen Kulttheologie und ihren Voraussetzungen." *ZAW* 70 (1958), 59–98.

Dunn, J. D. G. *Romans 1–8.* WBC. Dallas: Word Books, 1988.

————. *Romans 9–16.* WBC. Dallas: Word Books, 1988.

Eissfeldt, O. *Die Composition der Samuelisbücher.* Leipzig: Hinrichs, 1931.

Ellul, J. *The Politics of God and the Politics of Man.* Grand Rapids: Eerdmans, 1972.

Eslinger, L. *The Kingship of God in Crisis.* Sheffield, JSOT: 1985.

Fohrer, G. *Introduction to the Old Testament.* London: SPCK, 1970.

Gelston, A. "The Missionary Message of Second Isaiah." *SJT* 18 (1965), 308–18.

Gibson, J. C. L. *Canaanite Myths and Legends.* 2d ed. Edinburgh: T. and T. Clark, 1978.

Goldingay, John. *Approaches to Old Testament Interpretation.* 2d ed. Leicester: Apollos, 1990.

_____. *Theological Diversity and the Authority of the Old Testament.* Grand Rapids: Eerdmans, 1987.

Good, E. M. *Irony in the Old Testament.* London: SPCK, 1965.

Gordon, R. P. *1 and 2 Samuel.* Old Testament Guides. Sheffield: JSOT, 1984.

_____. *1 and 2 Samuel: A Commentary.* Exeter: Paternoster, 1986.

Gottwald, N. K. *The Tribes of Yahweh.* Maryknoll, NY: Orbis, 1979.

Gray, J. *I and II Kings.* 3d ed. OTL. London: SCM, 1977.

Gros Louis, K. R. R. "The Book of Judges." Pp. 141–62 in K. Gros Louis, J. Ackerman, T. Warshaw, eds., *Literary Interpretations of Biblical Narratives.* Nashville: Abingdon, 1974.

Gunkel, H. *Genesis.* Göttingen: Vandenhoeck and Ruprecht, 1902.

Gunn, D. M. *The Fate of King Saul: An Interpretation of a Biblical Story.* Sheffield: JSOT, 1980.

_____. "New Directions in the Study of Biblical Hebrew Narrative." *JSOT* 39 (1987), 65–75. *The Story of King David.* Sheffield: JSOT, 1978.

Halbe, J. "Gemeinschaft, die Welt unterbricht." Pp. 55–75 in N. Lohfink, ed., *Das Deuteronomium.*

Haran, M. *Temples and Temple Service in Ancient Israel.* Oxford: Oxford University Press, 1978.

Hobbs, T. R. *2 Kings.* WBC. Waco: Word Books, 1985.

_____. *1 and 2 Kings.* WBT. Dallas: Word Books, 1989.

Hoelscher, G. "Komposition und Ursprung des Deuteronomiums." *ZAW* 40 (1922), 161–255.

Hoffmann, H.-D. *Reform und Reformen: Untersuchungen zu einem Grundthema der deuteronomistischen Geschichtsschreibung.* Zurich: Theologischer Verlag, 1980.

Hoftijzer, J. *Die Landverheissungen an die drei Erzväter.* Leiden: Brill, 1956.

Holladay, W. L. *Jeremiah 2.* Hermeneia. Minneapolis: Fortress, 1989.

Horst, F. *Das Privilegrecht Jahves.* Göttingen: Vandenhoeck and Ruprecht, 1930.

Janssen, E. *Juda in der Exilszeit: Ein Beitrag zur Frage der Entstehung des Judentums.* Göttingen: Vandenhoeck and Ruprecht, 1956.

Jobling, D. *The Sense of Biblical Narrative.* Vol. 1. Sheffield: JSOT, 1978.

Kitchen, K. A. *Ancient Orient and Old Testament.* London: Tyndale Press, 1966.

Klein, Lillian R. *The Triumph of Irony in the Book of Judges.* Sheffield: Sheffield Academic Press, 1988.

Klein, R. W. *1 Samuel.* WBC. Waco: Word Books, 1983.

Kline, M. G. *The Treaty of the Great King.* Grand Rapids: Eerdmans, 1963.

Koorevaar, H. J. *De Opbouw van het Boek Jozua.* Heverlee: Centrum voor Bijbelse Vorming Belgie v. z. w., 1990.

Kugel, J. L. *The Idea of Biblical Poetry.* New Haven: Yale University Press, 1981.

Lindblom, J. *Prophecy in Ancient Israel.* Oxford: Blackwell, 1962.

Lohfink, N., ed. *Das Deuteronomium: Entstehung, Gestalt und Botschaft.* Leuven: Leuven University Press, 1965.

_____. *Das Hauptgebot: Eine Untersuchung literarischer Einleitungsfragen zu Dtn 5–11.* Rome: Biblical Institute Press, 1963.

_____. *Die Landverheissung als Eid.* Stuttgart: Katholisches Bibelwerk, 1967.

_____. "Die Bundesurkunde des Königs Josias." *Biblica* 44 (1963), 261–88, 461–98.

_____. "Die deuteronomische Darstellung des Übergangs der Führung Israels von Moses auf Josua." *Scholastik* 37 (1962), 32–44.

_____. "Zur neueren Diskussion über 2 Kön 22–23." Pp. 24–48 in N. Lohfink, ed., *Das Deuteronomium.*

Long, V. P. *The Reign and Rejection of King Saul.* Atlanta: Scholars Press, 1989.

Mayes, A. D. H. *Deuteronomy.* NCB. London: Oliphants, 1979.

_____. *Judges.* OT Guides. Sheffield: JSOT, 1985.

————. *The Story of Israel from Settlement to Exile*. London: SCM, 1983.

Mendenhall, G. E. "Ancient Oriental and Biblical Law." *BA* 17 (1954), 26–46.

————. "Covenant Forms in Israelite Tradition." *BA* 17 (1954), 50–76.

Merendino, R. P. *Das Deuteronomische Gesetz*. Bonn: P. Hanstein, 1969.

Milgrom, J. "The Alleged 'Demythologization' and 'Secularization' in Deuteronomy." *IEJ* 23 (1973), 151–56.

Miller, P. D. *Deuteronomy*. Interpretation. Louisville: John Knox, 1990.

Minette de Tillesse, G. "Sections 'Tu' et Sections 'Vous' dans le Deuteronome." *VT* 12 (1962), 29–87.

Mittmann, S. *Deuteronomium 1:1–6:3 literarkritisch und traditionsgeschichtlich untersucht*. Berlin: de Gruyter, 1975.

Moehlenbrink, K. "Die Landnahmasagen des Buches Josua." *ZAW* 15 (1936), 236–68.

McCarter, P. K. *I Samuel*. AB. New York, Doubleday, 1980.

McCarter, P. K. *II Samuel*. AB. New York, Doubleday, 1984.

McCarthy, D. J. "II Samuel 7 and the Structure of the Deuteronomic History." *JBL* 84 (1965), 131–38.

————. *Treaty and Covenant*. Rome, Pontifical Biblical Institute, 1978 (second edition).

McConville, J. G. *Law and Theology in Deuteronomy*. Sheffield, JSOT, 1984.

————. "The Shadow of the Curse: A Key to Old Testament Theology." *Evangel* 3/1 (1985), 2–5.

————. "Narrative and Meaning in the Books of Kings." *Biblica* 70 (1989), 31–49.

————. "Jeremiah: Prophet and Book." *TB* 42 (1991), 80–95.

————. "1 Kings VIII 46–53 and the Deuteronomic Hope." *VT* 42 (1992), 67–79.

————. *Judgment and Promise: Interpreting the Book of Jeremiah*. Winona Lake, Ind.: Eisenbrauns/ IVP (UK), 1993.

McKane, W. "Relations Between Poetry and Prose in the Book of Jeremiah with Special Reference to Jeremiah III 6–11 and XII 14–17." *SVT* 32 (1980), 220–37.

Nelson, R. D. *The Double Redaction of the Deuteronomistic History.* Sheffield: JSOT, 1981.

Nicholson, E. W. *Deuteronomy and Tradition.* Oxford: Blackwell, 1967.

———. *Preaching to the Exiles: A Study of the Prose Tradition in the Book of Jeremiah.* Oxford: Blackwell, 1970.

———. *God and His People.* Oxford: Clarendon, 1986.

Noth, M. *The Deuteronomistic History.* Sheffield: JSOT, 1981. English translation of *Überlieferungsgeschichtliche Studien.* 2d ed. Tübingen: Niemayer, 1957, 1–110.

———. *A History of Pentateuchal Traditions.* Englewood Cliffs, N.J.: Prentice Hall, 1972.

———. *Das System der zwölf Stämme Israels.* Stuttgart: Kohlhammer, 1930.

———. "David and Israel in II Samuel VII." Pp. 250–59 in his *The Laws in the Pentateuch and Other Studies.*

———. "The Understanding of History in Old Testament Apocalyptic." Pp. 194–214 in his *The Laws in the Pentateuch and Other Studies.* London: SCM, 1966.

Paul, M. J. *Het Archimedisch Punt van de Pentateuchkritiek.* Gravenhage: Uitgeverij Boekencentrum, 1988.

Perlitt, L. *Bundestheologie im alten Testament.* Neukirchen: Neukirchener Verlag, 1969.

———. "Deuteronomium 1–3 im Streit der exegetischen Methoden." Pp. 149–63 in N. Lohfink ed., *Das Deuteronomium.*

Petersen, D. L. *The Roles of Israel's Prophets.* Sheffield: JSOT, 1981.

Polzin, R. *Moses and the Deuteronomist.* New York: Seabury, 1980.

———. *Samuel and the Deuteronomist.* San Francisco: Harper and Row, 1989.

Preuss, H. D. *Deuteronomium.* Darmstadt: Wissenschaftliche Buchgesellschaft, 1982.

Pritchard, J. B. *Ancient Near Eastern Texts Relating to the Old Testament.* Princeton: Princeton University Press, 1969.

Provan, I. W. *Hezekiah and the Books of Kings.* Berlin: de Gruyter, 1988.

Puukko, F. *Das Deuteronomium: Eine literarkritische Untersuchung.* Leipzig, 1910.

Rad, G. von. *Deuteronomy.* OTL. London: SCM, 1966.

———. *Das Gottesvolk.* Stuttgart: Kohlhammer, 1929.

_____. *Old Testament Theology*. 2 vols. London: Oliver and Boyd, 1962, 1965.

_____. *Studies in Deuteronomy*. London: SCM, 1953.

_____. "The Form-Critical Problem of the Hexateuch." Pp. 1–78 in von Rad's *The Problem of the Hexateuch and Other Essays*. London: SCM, 1984.

_____. "The Beginnings of Historical Writing in Ancient Israel." Pp. 166–204 in von Rad's *The Problem of the Hexateuch and Other Essays*.

Richter, W. *Traditionsgeschichtliche Untersuchungen zum Richterbuch*. Bonn: P. Hanstein, 1963.

_____. *Die Bearbeitung des "Retterbuches" in der deuteronomistischen Epoche*. Bonn: P. Hanstein, 1964.

Rose, M. *Der Ausschliesslichkeitsanspruch Jahwehs*. Stuttgart: Kohlhammer, 1975.

Rost, L. *The Succession to the Throne of David*. Sheffield: Almond, 1982. First German edition, Stuttgart: Kohlhammer, 1926.

Schmid, H. H. *Gerechtigkeit als Weltordnung*. Tübingen, J. C. B. Mohr, 1968.

Seitz, G. *Redaktionsgeschichtliche Studien zum Deuteronomium*. Stuttgart: Kohlhammer, 1971.

Skweres, D. E. *Die Rückverweise im Buch Deuteronomiums*. Rome: Biblical Institute Press, 1979.

Smend, R. "Das Gesetz und die Voelker." Pp. 494–509 in H. W. Wolff, ed. *Probleme Biblischer Theologie*. Munich: Kaiser, 1971.

Soggin, J. A. *Judges*. OTL. London: SCM, 1981.

Spieckermann, H. *Juda unter Assur in der Sargonidenzeit*. Göttingen: Vandenhoeck and Ruprecht, 1982.

Staerk, W. *Beiträge zur Kritik des Deuteronomiums*. Leipzig, 1894.

Steuernagel, C. *Deuteronomium und Josua*. HKAT. Göttingen: Vandenhoeck and Ruprecht, 1900.

Stulman, L. *The Prose Sermons of the Book of Jeremiah*. SBLDS 83. Atlanta: Scholars Press, 1986.

Thiel, W. *Die deuteronomistische Redaktion von Jeremia 1–25*. Neukirchen: Neukirchener Verlag, ·1973.

Thompson, J. A. *Deuteronomy*. TOTC. London: IVP, 1974.

Van Seters, J. *In Search of History*. New Haven: Yale University Press, 1983.

Vannoy, J. R. *Covenant Renewal at Gilgal: A Study of 1 Samuel 11:14–12:25*. Easton, Pa.: Mack Publishing Co., 1978.

Veijola, T. *Die Ewige Dynastie*. Helsinki: Suomalainen Tiedeakatemia, 1975.

————. *Das Königtum in der Beurteilung der deuteronomistischen Historiographie*. Helsinki, Suomalainen Tiedeakatemia, 1977.

Webb, B. G. *The Book of the Judges*. Sheffield: JSOT, 1987.

Weinfeld, M. *Deuteronomy and the Deuteronomic School*. Oxford: Clarendon, 1972.

————. "The Emergence of the Deuteronomic Movement: The Historical Antecedents." Pp. 76–98 in N. Lohfink, ed. *Das Deuteronomium*.

Weippert, H. *Die Prosareden des Jeremiabuches*. Berlin: de Gruyter, 1973.

Welch, A. C. *The Code of Deuteronomy*. London, J. Clarke, 1924.

————. *Deuteronomy: The Framework to the Code*. London: Oxford University Press, 1932.

Wellhausen, J. *Die Composition des Hexateuchs und der historischen Bücher des alten Testaments*. 2d ed. Berlin: Georg Reimer, 1889.

————. *Prolegomena to the History of Ancient Israel*. Edinburgh: A. and C. Black, 1885.

Wenham, G. J. "Deuteronomy and the Central Sanctuary." *TB* 22 (1971), 113–18.

Westermann, C. *Genesis 12–36*. London: SPCK/ Minneapolis: Augsburg, 1985.

de Wette, W. M. L. *Dissertatio critico-exegetica qua Deuteronomium a prioribus pentateuchi libris diversum, alius cuiusdam recentioris auctoris opus esse monstratur*. Jena, 1805.

Wilson, R. R. *Prophecy and Society in Ancient Israel*. Philadelphia: Fortress, 1980.

Wiseman, D. J. *The Vassal Treaties of Esarhaddon*. London: British School of Archaeology in Iraq, 1958.

Wolff, H. W. "Hoseas geistige Heimat." Pp. 232-50 in his *Gesammelte Studien zum alten Testament*. Munich: Kaiser Verlag, 1964.

————. "Das Kerygma des deuteronomistischen Geschichtswerks." *ZAW* 73 (1961), 171–186. English trans.: pp. 83–100 in W. Brueggemann and Wolff, ed., *The Vitality of the Old Testament Traditions*. Richmond, Va.: John Knox, 1975.

BIBLIOGRAPHY

Wright, C. J. H. *God's People in God's Land: Family, Land and Property in the Old Testament*. Grand Rapids: Eerdmans, 1990.

Wright, G. E. "The Lawsuit of God: A Form-critical Study of Deuteronomy 32." Pp. 26–67 in B. W. Anderson ed., *Israel's Prophetic Heritage*. New York: Harper & Row, 1962.

Wright, N. T. *The Messiah and the People of God*. Ph.D. dissertation, Oxford University, 1980.

Younger, K. L. *Ancient Conquest Accounts: A Study in Ancient Near Eastern and Biblical History Writing*. Sheffield: JSOT, 1990.

◆ Author Index ◆

AUTHOR INDEX

Lindblom, J., 129
Lohfink, N., 17, 30, 38, 41, 46, 59, 62, 80, 84
Long, V. P., 70, 114

McCarter, P. K., 127
McCarthy, D. J., 58f.
McConville, J. G., 12, 18f., 26, 49, 53f., 56, 60, 66, 76, 78, 80, 82, 90f., 99, 131, 133, 144, 148
McKane, W., 56, 66, 83
Mayes, A. D. H., 38f., 54, 59f., 69, 80, 93, 96f., 102, 106f., 109, 111ff., 135
Mendenhall, G. E., 28, 57f.
Merendino, R. P., 18
Milgrom, J., 48
Minette de Tillesse, G., 37, 41, 57
Mittmann, S., 35f., 39
Moehlenbrink, K., 100

Nelson, R. D., 87
Nicholson, E. W., 22f., 27f., 30, 43, 55, 58f., 129f.
Noth, M., 11, 16, 34f., 37, 39f., 44, 48, 54, 57, 67, 69, 72, 76, 78f., 85, 89, 91ff., 95f., 98, 102f., 109, 111f.

Perlitt, L., 40, 44, 46, 57, 61ff.
Petersen, D. L., 26
Polzin, R., 74, 95ff., 102, 121
Preuss, H. D., 37, 60f.
Provan, I., 79ff.
Puukko, F., 34

Rad, G. von, 20ff., 27, 33f., 41, 43, 46f., 54, 59, 72, 77f., 99, 113, 129, 146

Richter, W., 69
Rose, M., 35f., 38f.
Rost, L., 70f., 116

Seitz, G., 38f
Schmid, H. H., 131
Smend, R., 40, 83ff., 93, 97, 104, 138
Soggin, J. A., 69, 100, 109
Spieckermann, H., 84
Staerk, W., 37
Steuernagel, C., 18, 34, 37
Stulman, L., 66
Sykes, S., 13f.

Thiel, W., 56, 66, 83

Vannoy, J. R., 115
Van Seters, J., 71, 133f.
Veijola, T., 56, 83f.

Webb, B., 76, 78, 104ff.
Weinfeld, M., 17, 19, 25, 27, 29f., 32, 48, 56, 58, 131
Weippert, H., 56
Welch, A. C., 27, 51, 53f.
Wellhausen, J., 10, 16ff., 22f., 34, 40, 112, 129, 135
Wenham, G. J., 54
Westermann, C., 47
Wette, W. M. L. de, 10, 15
Whybray, H., 71
Wilson, R. R., 26, 66
Wiseman, D. J., 58
Wolff, H., 20, 83, 89
Wright, C. J. H., 70
Wright, G. E., 51
Wright, N. T., 152

Younger, K. L., 94f., 97f., 102

◆ Subject Index ◆

◆ Acknowledgments ◆

I am grateful to the Council of Tyndale House, Cambridge, for sponsoring the writing of this book by a generous grant. This was made possible by an arrangement with my employers, Wycliffe Hall, Oxford. I am grateful also to my colleagues, therefore, for ensuring that I had the time to complete the manuscript in the course of a busy academic year.